FIGARO HERE, FIGARO THERE

FIGARO HERE, FIGARO THERE

Pavilion Opera: An Impresario's Diary

Freddie Stockdale

Illustrations by the author

JOHN MURRAY

Text and illustrations © Freddie Stockdale 1991

First published in 1991
by John Murray (Publishers) Ltd
50 Albemarle Street, London W1X 4BD

The moral right of the author has been asserted

British Library Cataloguing in Publication Data
Stockdale, Freddie
   Figaro Here, Figaro There: Pavilion Opera: an
impresario's diary.
I. Title
792.50941

ISBN 0-7195-4970-1

Typeset by Rowland Phototypesetting Ltd,
Bury St Edmunds, Suffolk
Printed in Great Britain at the
University Press, Cambridge

To Joanna

In writing this book I am greatly indebted to Bryan Evans, Rosalind Hanbury, Christine Baxter, Caroline Knox and Kate Chenevix Trench for their constant patience and forthright advice, and to my sons Harry, Alexander and Valentine for their support and forbearance.

Introduction

Driving back from Anglesey with Figaro and Susanna, I was so tired I could hardly see the road.

'For heaven's sake, say something to wake me up.'

Figaro opened one eye. 'Did you know there was a vote on whether to go on strike at Elton Hall?'

Taking opera to other people's houses, in Brentford or Karachi, is a wonderful way of life. You see the best and the worst of a bizarre mixture of people with one glorious common denominator – they are all crazy enough to plunge into the operatic cauldron. 'Planes are missed, sopranos shriek, tenors bridle, door handles come off in your hand – but at the climax when the music fills the room and all are rapt, you could forgive them anything.

Delnadamph is the name of a small valley in Scotland. The river Don rises there in the peat flats below the Cairngorms and for thirty years it was my home. In the summer we fished the Don and the Cock Burn for trout, later we drove the grouse round the hills and crept along the river banks to surprise the wild duck. In the autumn, long days, from pre-dawn to post-dusk, were spent stalking the stags on the tops and in the steep corries running up towards Ben More. Delnadamph means 'Valley of the Deer' and it was Paradise. With a flaw. You had to like killing.

When I finally rebelled, I sold the property and found myself in the unusual position of being able to pay off my overdraft *and* build a very small opera pavilion in the garden. I engaged a Musical Director, six singers and a producer, and together we spent an idyllic month in Lincolnshire rehearsing *Così fan tutte*. We put on six performances, sold 352 tickets and gave away another 100. People in the audience asked if we would take our production on tour. So in 1982 nine of us put on 22 performances in 8 houses. In 1991 there are 30 of us putting on

125 performances, visiting 100 houses in 12 countries. This book is an accurate portrait of a typical year. Some names have been changed to protect the guilty.

October 1

Everyone has a moment they would rather forget. Mine is of standing up at a London conference on penal reform and calling out 'Mr Question! I should like to ask a Chairman'. It says something about penal reformers that this contribution was heard with respectful attention. Nevertheless, I am now wary of speaking in public.

But sometimes there's no way of avoiding it: last night we were putting on *Don Pasquale* at Gray's Inn, and Graham (Ernesto) was off with a sore throat.

'Ladies and Gentleman!'

Chatter, chatter; I had another go.

'LADIES AND GENTLEMEN!'

'Sh!' 'He's trying to say something.' 'Be quiet, darling.'

'Tonight, the role of Ernesto . . .'

'WE CAN'T HEAR!'

It's an absolute nightmare.

It's harder to explain what we do than why we do it (love of opera and money). You've got to imagine a large drawing-room, say twenty-five feet square. Apart from a grand piano in front of the fireplace, there are three rows of people seated round the rest of the room, all four sides, with their backs to the walls. This leaves a hollow rectangle in the middle of the room. I hope this will measure twelve feet by eighteen, which is the size of my Indian carpet on which the stories of the operas unfold: love affairs, family rows, and sword fights. If it's bigger, hooray; if it's smaller, there may be unintentional casualties. If people in the audience are looking bemused or threatened, it means they've never been before and are unaccustomed to staring straight into other people's faces across such a narrow divide. Indeed, who could blame them?

Punctually every evening Bryan Evans, pianist and musical director, walks quietly in – to roars of applause if they know him, to embarrassed silence if they don't. He's never missed a

show in eleven years. He tries to cheer me up with a smile, the
lights fade and wham! he attacks the piano with terrific gusto.
What's happened to the orchestra? We got rid of them after
hearing them at the first dress rehearsal, back in 1981: Bryan
played instead, and eight hundred performances later he's still
playing, chained to the keyboard by an anxious impresario. In
come the characters. They're in period dress – probably the same
period as the room. Using a piano promotes the vocal line; they
soar into a duet, the audience start to relax. Pavilion Opera is
getting on with the job.

Tonight: *Così fan tutte*. It was nice to see an old friend in the
audience – Miss Bruell, doyenne of dieticians and a great
benefactor to all my children. Unfortunately, she had propped
her umbrella up against the curtain blinds. Despina (the maid)
swept in and raised the blinds one by one, by pulling on the
cords. Up they went – the last carrying Miss Bruell's umbrella
to a point ten feet above her head. I didn't see this immediately,
but I could see some of the audience beginning to smile.
Suddenly half the people in the room were rolling about, while
the other half stared back in complete mystification, indeed
growing alarm. The more our side laughed, the more the other
side began to twitch. Bryan and I had now seen the umbrella,
poised above its owner and looking distinctly dangerous. The

cast were of course completely unaware, and carried on singing the duet with grim determination. Then Miss Bruell noticed her umbrella was missing, and began to feel about surreptitiously under her chair while pretending to concentrate on the opera. This was too much for those facing her. One man looked as if he was going to be sick. At last Despina spotted the problem and briskly let down the blind, which deposited the umbrella with a sharp crack at Miss Bruell's side. She looked surprised, but grateful. We should keep her in the show every night.

October 2

We try to work (or travel) six days a week. It's my fault, and my financial loss, if we don't. Tonight is a blank in our diary, and I was taken by some friends to Covent Garden. It's a magical place, and whatever I have learnt about opera comes from the Golden Age there of Drogheda and Solti. Night after night, thanks to a generous mother, I soaked up Gobbi as Scarpia, Sutherland as Norma, Minton as Octavian. It was heaven. But tonight, Donizetti's *Lucia di Lammermoor* provided a perfect example of why Pavilion Opera (a minor diversion in the world of mainstream opera) was ever started. The great love duet approached. On the stage above us, a massive woman strode forward and let out a terrible bellow. Be he lord of never so many primeval swamps, surely the stoutest mastodon would have quailed before such a mate. And yet – a tiny, round little man, his pudgy arms aflap, lolloped on and took his place beside her. Neither looked at the other (just as well, some might say); both stared at the conductor as they screamed out their undying passion.

Sheltering in the stalls, I thought as always how poor a representation of real life a performance such as this is. You and I know that we look our love in the face as we tell her or him those things we wish to communicate. Does good acting have to be sacrificed to the music? I don't think so. But as long as the prevailing custom continues among the big houses of employing only the oldest surviving interpreter of any given role (because they are familiar through past recordings), so long will smaller enterprises be able to find beautiful Susannas and slender Alfredos.

October 3

The whole thing started a long while ago. I spent much of my time at Eton gazing with increasing affection at successive stained glass windows by John Piper, and most of my law lectures at Cambridge sketching imaginary palaces. I wasted most of the next few years farming with more enthusiasm than common sense, and destroying such wildlife as came my way. In those days I was still married, and we used to put on concerts in the house when the neighbours came to dinner. It was one way of avoiding the re-run of the saga of what happened to that high partridge in the second drive after lunch.

By 1978 I had become keen to try a small opera production to put my ideas of intimate, realistic story-telling into effect, and the idea had grown of combining this with the Piper-and-palaces influences. My original plan was to build an opera pavilion at the end of a new lime avenue centred on the house with another, smaller, pavilion serving as a swimming-pool summer-house.

The architect Francis Johnson is a heroic figure. Working from a large set of minutely detailed diaries drawn during his architectural travels, he has kept the standard of classical architecture flying in the north of England for fifty years while all about him were careering down the primrose path of steel windows and concrete blocks. His rallying call has always been 'Classical achitecture is no more expensive!' and the recent award of the CBE to coincide with his eightieth birthday seems scarcely adequate for what his life has achieved so far.

Anyway, he had already built a lodge for me in Scotland and I felt we worked well together. He has a bias towards dignified austerity, I incline towards undignified excess. Our meeting point may therefore hope to be rich, but restrained.

We corresponded for 18 months about the design and then one day, a mechanical digger arrived in the field and work began, a mere 50 yards from my bedroom window. In the meantime I had made contact with John Piper. We shared a mutual friend in my neighbour, the Reverend Henry Thorold, a Lincolnshire squarson whose generous proportions are more than matched by his imagination and hospitality.

Dining at Marston, his home, I was drawn towards the fireplace in the hall, all that remains of a medieval manor house.

'Another glass of hock?' he asked solicitously.

'Yes, please,' I said. 'Is John Piper still alive?'

'STILL ALIVE?' Henry's years of preaching in the great Anglo-Catholic chapel at Lancing had not been wasted. 'STILL ALIVE?'

'Well, is he?'

'STILL ALIVE?' he roared with galactic laughter. 'OF COURSE he's still alive. Why, he's coming to stay with me next month.'

This was exciting news. 'Does he still design glass?'

'STILL DESIGN GLASS?'

So we arranged a rendezvous.

One of my favourite windows in Eton College Chapel included the effect, when the sun reached a certain point relative to my seat, of projecting a piercing shaft of dazzling light straight into my left eye. I had always assumed that this portrayed Paul's conversion on the road to Damascus. But, when asked, the verger assured me it was the parable of the raising of Lazarus.

'Have you ever done the life of Paul?' I asked John Piper when we met. 'Never', he replied. So we settled on The Stoning of St Stephen, The Road to Damascus, The Shipwreck at Malta and the Beheading at Trifontium, after finally rejecting The Letting Down in the Basket in favour of the seascape. It was only after they were completed that his wife, Myfanwy, pointed out that each window contained a separate element: Earth, Air, Fire, Water. It was a thrilling moment when the designs were first unveiled.

But back to the after-dinner concert days. We were going to have some Mozart. In walked a quiet, dark, bespectacled young man with a simply ravishing girl: Bryan Evans and his then fiancée, Rebecca Moseley-Morgan. She was going to sing, and he was going to accompany her on my new piano, an instrument so stiff you needed a sledgehammer to make it respond.

'I'm afraid my page-turner couldn't come,' he said. Well, thank God for that, I thought. I wasn't sure we had enough bedrooms.

'Who could do it?' he asked.

'What?'

'Turn my pages.' This was my first glimpse of the Evans grin – deceptively mild, it means 'I'm telling you what to do, but I'd rather do it in a friendly way'. (The singers freeze when he grins at them in a performance. They say it's like suddenly spotting an alligator.)

'I'll do it,' I said. 'I'm afraid I can't read music.'

'Just follow the words.' He grinned again. 'I'll nudge you if you get it wrong.'

It was terrifying. I hated being, as it were, on display before the audience. But once he started to play, it was also exhilarating. The music swept every other emotion away. And when Rebecca, eyes sparkling, opened her lips and filled the rooms with Zerlina's sex-appeal, even old Potter Simpson, scourge of Lincolnshire's lowest pheasants, was enthralled.

'I bet she's a goer!' he confided afterwards, thereby alerting me to a potential selling point for Pavilion Opera – as it already was, in my mind. If the sopranos are pretty, and appear willing on stage, half the audience will get a very considerable charge. Match them with sultry, enigmatic tenors and the whole room will be in an uproar. That's show business! (It wasn't long before I discovered the flaw: there aren't any sultry, enigmatic tenors.)

Potter Simpson takes a "low one"

The evening was a great success. I had Rebecca on my right at supper. There were many questions I wanted to ask her. She could hardly speak because of a sore throat, and her little face swam above a thick cashmere choker.

'Would it be possible to recruit some of your colleagues to do a performance of *Così fan tutte*?' I asked.

'Here?' she croaked. Isn't it curious that you can sing with a bad throat, yet hardly speak?

'Well, there . . .' I pointed airily across the lawn towards the low and level fen stretching far away. 'We're building a pavilion' I said, adding '– not the sort with a thatched roof', in case she thought it was for cricket. She was looking rather wary. Bryan moved round to join us.

And it was agreed. They would supply the professional cast. I would find a semi-amateur orchestra. August 1981 would see us all working together.

And it happened. The walls of the pavilion began to rise. Every day I woke up to the sound of bricks being tapped into place, and later to the sawing of timbers and the banging of hammers. It was an invigorating time. Completion brought aching withdrawal symptoms. I had begun work on the swimming pool before I realized that building *two* pavilions would be beyond my resources, and I can quite understand why some people keep building up to and beyond bankruptcy. Even now, I am never so happy as when the house vibrates with repairs and the air stings with the scent of paint and varnish.

October 4

Although we're hard at work on tour, there's pressure in the company for decisions about next year's contract. This year we're doing *Così, Lucia, Don Pasquale, Fledermaus* and *Traviata*. Next year it will be *Figaro, Barber, Don Giovanni* and *Rigoletto*.

Auditions all day today. We start at nine, which is very hard on the aspiring singers. But with 400 to hear each year, we have to try to fit in forty a day: ten minutes each, to hear one aria and then discuss it afterwards. If they choose a short one, we're away. If they go for one of opera's great unfulfilled promises, 'Parto, parto' from *La Clemenza di Tito* (roughly the equivalent of the politician's phrase 'And finally . . .') – then we're in trouble.

Picture the scene: the two of us sitting unassumingly on a sofa while some gorgeous girl pirouettes in front of us, singing like a lark. Reluctantly, we part from her.

ME: 'She's wonderful.'

BRYAN *looks thoughtfully at his feet.*

ME: 'You *must* admit – she'd be a stunning Susanna.'

BRYAN: 'It's your company.'

ME (*defeated*): 'Let's hear the next one.'

Performing six nights a week, as we try to do, we need two good singers for each role in case someone is ill. Employers and their audiences are entitled to expect that the show can survive a sore throat or two. We once did a show at Capesthorne, Blore's grimy red-brick adjustment of the much older Bromley Davenport seat in Cheshire, with nine of the principals off with 'flu. There was hardly anyone on stage singing their original role and it took me five minutes to read out the cast changes. The marvellous thing is that audiences really warm to struggling last-minute replacements. An understudy can count on a lot of sympathetic support. The worst evening was *Così* at Somerset House. The baritone (Guglielmo – one of the two suitors) had fish poisoning. His cover had neglected his work quite disgracefully. He arrived late and it was soon apparent he had forgotten all the moves.

'Don't worry,' Ferrando, his colleague, told him. 'Just do what I do.'

We reached the point when the two lovers each select a mistress. Ferrando rushed over to Fiordiligi, sung by Alice, and knelt at her feet. Ignoring the other girl, the idiot Guglielmo also rushed over to Fiordiligi. Keeping admirably calm, she looked from one to the other with deliciously improvised uncertainty.

'What do you think *I* felt like?' her stage sister, Dorabella, asked me after the show.

I didn't tell her several of the audience had said they couldn't spot which was the understudy.

October 5

Today was Bayham. The stupendously ugly Scottish baronial 'Abbey' was abandoned in the seventies, and old Lord Camden's pretty neo-Georgian replacement has no large room. Hence a marquee. I had Helen and Noel, my two main singers, in my car.

'Who lives here?' he asked.

'Michael Pratt. We were at school together.' At this, the proprietor's face popped out of an upstairs window.

'Will you kindly move that car round to the back!'

I did as I was commanded. 'Did you say he was a friend?' whispered Helen.

The marquee was set up on a sloping lawn beyond a shallow ditch entitled the ha-ha. The problem with opera in marquees is

We're pretending nothing has happened.

that no one can hear. It is therefore vital to raise the seats so that some at least can see.

Hardly had the performance started when there was a loud crack from the raised line of seats to my right. It was occupied by a row of elderly patrons in evening dress. The whole stand had split in the middle, so that half the row was sharply angled one way, the other half perched at nearly ninety degrees towards them. All remained calm and expressionless with that special air English people adopt in a ridiculous position. In the occasional longueurs Bryan and I risked a glance at them, but in the end we had to stop because not one of them ever moved – they seemed frozen in dignified gloom.

October 6

Chesters, Northumberland. It seems to be one of those weeks. Two of the cast have been getting really fractious. There has been a lot of driving, and getting to this monumental heap of late-Victorian masonry on Hadrian's Wall has been a major task. The Bensons are so hospitable, I had thought the only problem was going to be their colossal and untuneable piano, which squats in the corner of the Library like a spider crouching to spring. They say it can't be moved. Indeed, this is the only justification for its presence. *However*, just before the show I was

warned that there would be a Company Meeting afterwards:
These meetings are a disastrous innovation in which the running
is made by whoever has a grievance; the others try to
concentrate on the roles they have to sing, but are inevitably
distracted. Well – employers can sometimes be saviours. The
great love duet went a bit flat, thanks to the gloomy emotions of
the two turtle-doves. When it comes to an end, they are
supposed to kiss ecstatically. Instead, they stared at one another
in stubborn silence. And into this silence came, from the back,
the booming voice of Colonel Benson:

'I *told* you it was your turn to worm the dogs.'

Ill-suppressed hysteria shook lovers and piano party; the
absolute indifference of the audience only made it worse. As
Bryan said afterwards, the really worrying thing was, what sort
of evidence could have given rise to such a remark. Anyway,
there was no more talk of a Meeting that night.

It's on difficult occasions that Bryan is such a support to me.
He is an intensely private person, which is why his appearance in
these pages will be less than his influence on me would otherwise
require. Born in Stockton, he studied piano at the Royal College
of Music, winning all the relevant prizes for Mozart, Chopin and
accompaniment. He became part of a piano trio, the Arion, and
started giving solo recitals here and abroad, mainly in Germany
and Austria. It was at this point, in 1978, that he accompanied
Rebecca to, and at, Thorpe Tilney. His apparently impermeable
façade of peaceable constraint hides a gloriously sharp wit and a
healthy sense of disregard for the pomp and bombast of other
people's self-promotion. It is a very rare combination: a
perfectionist artistry in his music and humorous self-deprecation
in his daily life.

Although Bryan is on excellent terms with all the singers, he
invariably gives me sound advice packed with ice-cold common
sense, something I rather lack. He has an unemotional ability to
see straight through a problem, ignoring the pretty packaging
designed to conceal its basic significance – or insignificance.

He is of medium height, with dark hair, and his glasses can

reflect the light in a slightly threatening manner. His ready smile and endless enthusiasm are very catching. He speaks very quietly – unlike the singers, who tend to bellow, I assume because of their highly developed vocal chords. Their laughter can silence a room.

October 7

Hutton-in-the-Forest. Now we're heading south. Pouring rain, some mist as we crossed the Pennines and came down to Penrith. Hutton is a fascinating amalgam of medieval pele tower, seventeenth-century Mannerism and Victorian bravura. Having managed to negotiate the lorry under the arch, I found the singers huddled in front of a façade entirely shuttered up. There was no sign of life at all. I rang the bell and hammered on the door. Nothing.

Then we heard footsteps dragging on the stone inside. Heavy bolts were drawn back, a chain rattled. Very, very slowly, the door opened with a Hammer House of Horrors creak, and old Lord Inglewood peered out.

'What do you want?' There was a note of panic in his voice.

He had obviously been enjoying a peaceful day in bed and it was an unpleasant task to break the news, not just that there were thirty of us needing to come in and set up an opera, but worse (since it was already five o'clock), that one hundred of his neighbours were even now bathing and changing to descend on him in two hours' time for a whole evening. Elsewhere, this community focus can make for a really good party. In lots of counties, our performance brings three ingredients together – raising money for a charity, meeting one's musically-minded friends, and seeing what fearful new misdecoration the Eastfinchampsteads have perpetrated in their drawing room. But tonight, I'm afraid this will have been small consolation.

October 8

I met John Cowasgee at the Zoo today. A friend of my
mother's, he wants us to do a show in Karachi to celebrate his
wedding anniversary. I had to ferry someone to a faith healer in
St John's Wood first, and the only suitable place to meet I could
think of was Regent's Park. There he was, an object of some
surprise to the queues of children, wearing a red carnation and
carrying *The Times*.

'You see,' he said, 'I've seen the same films.'

I'd missed lunch, so we found a Viennese cake shop in
Fitzrovia and tucked into coffee–cake with almond icing while
agreeing to terms and dates.

'But why is it more expensive than in London?'

'John. *Please*. Air fares?'

October 9

Our stage manager Kitty is super-efficient. She looks like
Carmen, with long black locks, slinky black blouses and jeans,
and a sultry expression. There's no trick to knowing when
anyone is out of favour with her. Tonight I was chatting to our
employers when she stalked over and started to complain about
something. This reminded me of an idea I had had, and later I
called everyone together.

'There's a new rule.' Silence.

'It's in everyone's interest.' Silence.

'From now on we all smile, even when we're cross about
something. We smile when the food is filthy. We smile when
we've forgotten something. We even smile during the curtain
calls, *please*,' I said. 'Thank you.' Impenetrably gloomy silence.
About par for a Company Meeting.

October 10

Well – the smiles are very much in evidence. Everyone's treating it as a joke, which works rather well. It's actually infectious; I find myself naturally smiling in return, and I'm sure there was a warmer response from the audience to the beaming cast. The minor exception is Kitty. She's smiling, all right – a wild, fixed, unearthly smile, decidedly ominous. With such a smile might Mrs Danvers have heard the de Winters' car approaching Manderley . . .

I'm still worrying about casting. Helen Kucharek, my prima donna, had to go on as Violetta in *Traviata* tonight, because the principal was away and the understudy, Alice, had lost her voice. Helen had never sung the role before, but bravely volunteered so as not to disappoint the audience.

So she sang it with the book. At the end, she put the score down (having memorized the last few bars), and we knew then that she was dying. It could have been ridiculous, but for some inexplicable reason it really affected me. She seemed to confront her fate with patient matter-of-fact acceptance, and there were several people in the audience in tears. It wasn't made easier by having Charlie Elwell among those present. An old friend, he sings himself and had come up to me before tea.

1.

2.

" from now on, smile !"

'I say, I'm longing to hear "Dei miei bollenti spiriti" tonight.'
To reinforce the point, he launched into it.

'Oh, good,' I said, privately hoping Graham was over his
cold. Anyway, we got to Act 2, Graham ambled on and opened
up with the great aria. He sang the first verse, and then he sang
the first verse again. Bryan and I exchanged glances. He sang the
first verse a third time. It's a good verse, an excellent verse in its
own way, and full of noble sentiments. But I knew that Bryan
was wondering how many times he was going to sing the
second verse, if indeed we ever reached it. Then suddenly
Graham stopped, gave us a terrible dying-duck look, and ran
from the room to tumultuous applause.

Charlie came up afterwards.

'What did you think of our rather idiosyncratic version?' I
asked nervously.

'Wonderful! It was wonderful!' he pumped my arm. 'The best
ever, and I've heard every recording there is. Where do you find
these singers?'

Where indeed?

October 11

Lucia at Cricket, a nice solid stone mansion made famous by two
television series of 'To the Manor Born'. Rosemary Taylor is a
pattern employer. She organizes our accommodation
meticulously, sells all her tickets well in advance, feeds us with
masses of hot food, pours wine down our throats after the show,
keeps smiling, and *never* complains. This may have something to
do with suffering seriously from a chronic bad back.

The architectural *coup de théâtre* about Cricket is that the whole
centre of the house is given over to a gigantic imperial staircase.
Few operas are not enhanced by having the steps sweeping down
in mid-aria, and the problem here of course is to keep the singers
off the staircase. Lucia creeping down in the half light, clutching

a carving knife and drenched in blood, was sensational.

This evening I've got my eldest son Harry with me, just back from corps camp. As Rosemary always has lots of young in the audience, this is a bonus for him.

And James Mason, whose final speech of thanks is delivered each year with the eloquence of Cicero. The famously silky villain? Not at all – the yet more famous but far from villainous silk.

Tonight he was as good as ever. There's aren't too many jokes in *Lucia*, so his speech was a welcome antidote to the gloom and gore.

October 12

Petworth. It's such a wonderful house – in some ways my favourite. That long plain front is so beautiful, a masterpiece of understated grandeur that is even more impressive than, say, the splendid exuberance of Castle Howard. It's a terrible thought that when the then Lord Leconfield consulted Salvin (star of Harlaxton and Thoresby), the great man examined the whole building and then said, shaking his head, 'I'm very sorry, my lord. The only way is to pull the whole thing down.' Luckily, this advice was ignored.

So was mine about the smile.

Kitty came into the White Library, all leather books and gilded furniture, where we were setting out the props for *Fledermaus*. There was some question about the stage management going off to get something in the town. Perhaps I should have been more flexible, but I needed everyone to assemble the lights. The next thing I knew, she had slammed the door with an ear-splitting crash. Do you know that feeling when rage bubbles up inside you and comes out like a geyser? I stood quite still for two or three seconds. Bryan said my face looked like a glass filling up with Ribena. Then I ran after her and, smiles forgotten, we had a fearful bellowing match in the hall.

But how many jobs would we get if we made a practice of smashing up people's houses?

October 13

It's pouring with rain, most of us have colds and the supper was filthy.

'You're very lucky. The caterer only got back from holiday today, specially to cook for you,' said Miss Curtis, our employer for the night.

'We all wish she'd stayed away. The food is cold, congealed and inedible and there was nothing for the vegetarians.'

'You shouldn't be so fussy.'

'I'm not fussy, and anyway it doesn't matter what I think. But you are contracted to feed these singers and they are entitled to a reasonable standard of food . . .'

Oh, how I dread mean employers. The flowers are wonderful. Champagne flows. But singers are servants, aren't they? They do it for fun. What are their *real* jobs?

Vegetarians *are* difficult. It *is* extra work. Not everyone sympathizes with them. But my experience is that easy people don't always make for great artists. If they sing beautifully, if they are fine stage managers, great costumiers, whatever – it's not such a big thing to ask, that they be given some fish to eat before a show. And they're *smiling*.

Our 43rd Consecutive Ham Salad.

October 14

Tomorrow we're off to Holland with *Fledermaus*, *Così*, *Lucia* and *Don Pasquale*, thanks to a Dutch friend, Reinier Baarsen, who persuaded me to try, and to the indefatigable Pico van Zoelen, who liked the idea and talked everybody else into doing it. Generations ago, Pico's family built an exquisite Baroque summer-house in a park near The Hague. Now he and his wife live in it – an excellent example of an eighteenth-century extravagance turning out to have been as shrewd an investment as any merchant venturing.

This morning we had more auditions. Some good, some bad.

Just before lunch two hunched characters shambled in, one to sing, the other to accompany him.

'These are the ones who particularly want you to listen to the pianist,' whispered Caroline, our auditions secretary.

Pom! . . . Pom! . . . Pom! . . .

Well, *I* certainly couldn't place those chords. I looked up.

Pom! . . . Pom! . . . Pom! . . .

Bryan's face was scarlet. I never, *never* laugh at auditions – but I felt those fatal palpitations that herald uncontrollable giggles. I looked at the floor. It didn't help. Then the singer opened his mouth. At once all desire to laugh faded. The sound was so dreadful, the murder of the music so violent, that we sat in chilled, humourless silence. On and on the voice ground – cracking and breaking and whining. It was so very sad. At last he left. We all stared at each other.

Osterley this evening. As soon as Lucia sang her first note tonight, I knew something was wrong. Instead of being clear, her voice sounded flawed, shadowy. Bryan's left eyebrow twitched – enough to show that he was gravely disturbed. I don't want to lose that singer, but knowing that Jeremy Isaacs from Covent Garden was lurking in the fifth row, discreetly camouflaged in a white dinner jacket, made me long for them all to excel. As he was too far back to see a thing, it was the voices that would count.

She croaked her way through 'Regnava nel silenzio', ignoring the crashes and bangs of Fred Metternich arriving late and breaking the arm off one of the mirror candelabras. He had a very pretty girl with him.

'Did you hear us?' she asked me timidly in the interval.

'No – would you like a trombone for the next act?'

Later, I stood at the door as the audience filed out. Mr Isaacs gave me a secret smile – so secret that afterwards I wondered if I had imagined it.

October 15

A good flight. The amount of clutter is unbelievable. Trunks, suitcases, several bags, and a big box of swords. Thirty of us, and four operas. Phyllida kept a place in the Heathrow queue. I watched the face of the man behind as the others joined her. He smiled at the first one, but gradually his face changed through horror to anger to complete disbelief. I wanted to sign him up. Pico's arrangements at Amsterdam were impeccable. He really has worked very hard to make this possible.

The odd thing about all this is that I never expected to do a second production. Contrary to the widespread assumption of my family and friends that I had discovered a new way of spending heaps of money, Così fan tutte, the first production, in 1981, did finally make a profit. But what impelled us forwards was the chance attendance of Ted Fawcett, the celebrated aesthete who ran the National Trust's musical programme. He was staying in Nottinghamshire and was brought over to the Pavilion for our last performance. It was the night that a storm rose which shook the country and, in the Channel, wrecked the Fastnet race. The audience ran through the puddles into the

Pavilion and huddled together while the wind whistled through the cracks and the rain beat against the glass. But they had the best of it. All August we had rehearsed, unthinkingly, in summer sunshine: several of the exits and entrances were arranged using the french windows giving on to the garden. It was too late to change this.

All evening drenched singers dashed in, panting and dripping, only to have to brace themselves before going out again to confront the elements. Those sitting near the doors began to turn blue, and to my horror I saw one man lean forward and bolt a door that kept blowing open. Was he mad? Didn't he realize what would happen? But I was trapped behind the piano. There was nothing I could do.

Slowly the soprano's aria built up to the point where the tenor was scheduled to join in. Sure enough, he came dashing round the corner into view, grabbed the door and found it locked. I could see his desperate face, a ghastly white through the sheets of rain. The soprano soared on – what could save us? He splashed to the next door, it opened, and he was in.

'Che bella giornata!' (What a delightful day!) I don't suppose da Ponte, the librettist, had envisaged this having any potential as a big laugh. He should have been there that night.

After we had navigated our way back to the house, I headed for the drinks tray.

'There's a man outside,' I was told.

'He must be *mad*!'

'He wants to see you.'

'Well, tell him to . . . no.' I changed my mind; after all, he must be pretty determined.

'I wondered,' asked Ted, once he had introduced himself and I had persuaded him to come into shelter, 'I wondered whether you would come and do a week for the National Trust in London next year, as part of our Festival?'

'All costs paid?' I'd learnt *something* from trying to milk cows in an arable area.

'How much?'

'Three thousand pounds,' I said firmly, hoping I'd got it right. 'Done.'

I picked up another six or seven houses by writing round, and so it went on for three years, growing slowly as entirely natural fears – '*Piano* opera? No *thanks*!' – were soothed by the combination of Bryan's mastery and the singers' cool professionalism.

It was not always easy with potential employers. I had chosen the people to write to from my copy of *Vitruvius Britannicus*. First I listed the houses with big enough rooms. Then I removed those whose owners I knew, since I thought it unfair to put them under pressure. Next I removed the known philistines – why waste a good stamp? Then I added one or two obvious examples of later houses not included in that majestic publication.

Some did not reply. Others asked to meet me, and I fell at that fence (my interview with Lord Montagu of Beaulieu lasted four minutes . . .).

Sir William Dugdale rang me up. 'How do I know your troupe is any good?'

'You don't,' I said. 'But would we waste your time if we weren't?'

'Not good enough,' he said, and rang off.

My own life was reaching a climactic season of change. Farming, a choice of career based on the delightful insouciance of life as it had appeared at home, was proving disastrously expensive. My marriage was plunging through armed neutrality towards outright war.

And then, in 1984/5, our order book doubled. I had increased the fees so that my hobby should make some small contribution towards the negative cash flow of my job. There was strong cause to keep away from home. My children, I reasoned, would cope better with an absent father, whether soldier, oil executive, or impresario, than with living in trenches hammered by the futile bombardments of the closing scenes of a marriage. So I took to the road. With no better way of spending my time, I visited every house that expressed an interest. When Jean Tilt, my cousin by digestion (our great-great-grandfathers ate the third member of the partnership they had set up to seek, and find, silver in the wilder west) invited me to New York, I accepted. Engagements in America and then Switzerland followed. By the end of 1988, we had chalked up five continents. This trip to Holland saw us well prepared.

October 16

Don Pasquale at Middachten, a beautiful red brick castle in a broad moat. No problems. Most of the company spent the night in and around Amsterdam, reporting strange sights.

So who's with the company here? Bryan of course, and Helen, and Helen's husband Noel, still in his twenties but in his seventh year with me. There's no part he won't attempt within his vocal range. He has made the role of Don Pasquale into a phenomenon – he just *becomes* a filthy old man, with alarming leer and arthritic gait, inside half an hour.

First, he detaches himself from the others and sits quietly, concentrating. Then he begins his make-up. Blotched red on the cheeks, a couple of teeth blacked out, lines, blemishes. The bottom teeth begin to protrude, the jaw sticks forward, a shoulder is half-hunched, the eyes become rheumy. He covertly ogles one of the girls, topless as she changes into her costume. Then the wig, all askew, the dirty old coat, with extra powder spilt on the shoulders. He stands up, slouching and repulsive. This is not a moment to ask him anything irrelevant. He is Don Pasquale now, not Noel Mann, and will remain so until after the performance. The show over, his face scrubbed with cold cream and that grimy impersonation mentally cast off, he reverts to a lean pale young man with a shatteringly loud laugh. People often ask him what part he played in the opera. It just never occurs to them that he might have been the old Don.

Alice, short, blonde, very beautiful, has a number of roles. Married (as I learnt much later) to a fellow Classicist at school with me twenty years ago, she is unmistakably from the southern United States. For me, she is the definitive Countess Almaviva in the *Marriage of Figaro*. She reads a lot, seldom speaks, and has a wide, bewitching smile. She is also very vague, often forgetting which opera we are supposed to be performing until the very last moment. I always expect her to launch into the wrong music, but so far she has only done it once, and that was in the middle of an aria so no one noticed except Bryan and me. Certainly not Alice.

'Whose version will you sing tonight, Alice?' I asked at the next performance.

'Why Fred-dee! What can you mean?'

'Oh . . . er . . . well . . .' It was no good. She'd never have believed me. It didn't happen again.

Blair is also from America. It was quite a battle to get him a work permit, but I had good friends who were willing to pester on my behalf. It probably is right to make employment here a distinct hurdle, but I feel that opera singers, like tennis players, are rather different from electricians or waitresses. Theirs is a short-term job and they are, by definition, chosen for their pre-eminent skills, not because they are cheaper and so undercut local talent. No one suggests that Wimbledon should be a perpetual battle between Martina Navratilova and Bjorn Borg. Young stars are positively welcomed.

The first day Blair came to the church hall we rent for rehearsals, he was followed ten minutes later by a policeman, who asked to speak to me. 'I'm sorry to bother you, sir,' he said, 'but I've had a report of a suspicious-looking person coming down here.'

Now, I look on the police as unmitigated Good News. They are, and always have been, a great source of personal reassurance. They often have to risk their lives to keep the rest of us free to do what we want. But this made me very angry. Blair is black, you see, and apparently this had made him, by definition, suspicious-looking to someone.

'Really? How can I help?'

'Can you vouch for everyone in here?' He was looking across the room at Blair.

'Yes,' I said. 'I can. Now please will you tell me what was so suspicious about this mystery character?' We stared at one another.

'I'm just following up on a report,' he said, and left.

We all of us felt ashamed.

While Blair takes the Mozartian tenor roles, Bruce Rankin takes the heavier heroic ones. His is a colossal, confident voice, that rings through a room. As the Duke of Mantua, or Edgardo, or Alfredo, he electrifies our audiences. What is nice for me is that we have forty-seven novels to talk about, since *he* loves Trollope, too. As does Susan Bisatt. She is our soprano, matching Bruce as Gilda or Lucia or Violetta. With a perfect classical profile, any designer's dream figure, and a wonderful capacity for capturing the alternating brazenness and pathos of our heroines, she will one day make a stupendous Tosca. I don't know if we can ever produce it, but I would cross an ocean to see her murder Scarpia.

And, of course, Enid, known as Mother because she is the kindest and most motherly girl in the company, always listening and helping where others may be more intent on expressing their own views. She is tiny, from New Zealand, of Italian descent, dark and pretty, never without scarlet lipstick. Her family know her only as Anne, which can lead to confusion.

And many others, because four productions entail chorus and understudies as well.

Every company has an informal grading system; if these are the stars, the second rank are no less important: Peter Blunt, for instance, tall, thin, curly-haired, rather sallow but with an enchanting smile, our all-purpose tenor, picking up the subsidiary roles with endless good humour, a great stand-by in tense moments. This is only his second year, but his natural thoughtfulness for others has made him quickly into an accepted member of the group. He seems settled into a cosy relationship with Emma, our number two mezzo soprano.

And Amy Montagu, slim, dark-eyed, masses of dark red hair and an enviably pure complexion, every impresario's dream soubrette. If her voice still lacks vocal power, her enthusiasm and natural magnetism earn her a place: Berta in the *Barber*, Flora in *Traviata*, Giannetta in *Elisir d'amore* – these are well within her range. Two more years and she will be a stunning Despina in *Così* or Susanna in *Figaro*. This is her first year out of college, yet she is already married to a rather dour figure who delivers her to rehearsals every morning and stands bleakly by the door each evening, waiting for her release. I've yet to introduce myself to him.

October 17

Lucia at Het Loo, the newly-restored palace originally built by William III and vastly enlarged by Napoleon's brother when he was briefly King of Holland. One of the problems in producing *Lucia* is how to stage the last act; as normally performed, it simply entails Edgardo moaning away about his Lucia being in another man's bed, and then stabbing himself when he hears that she is dying.

It has always seemed unconvincing. Dumas Fils wrote (in *La Dame aux Camélias*) that there is no pain worse than that felt by a man who believes that the woman he loves is in another's arms. I hope he's right! It doesn't seem to matter if she's there by force of duty or by deliberate choice — it's Painful. But enough for suicide?

However, the libretto gives Edgardo an equivocal line: 'You mean she's there?' This is usually done in classical pose, pointing heavenwards as the grisly old chaplain nods, confirming the news that she is dying.

But what if he's pointing downwards – to a coffin containing the dead body of his love? What if he wrenches open the lid and finds the corpse there, still warm? What if he lifts her hand, and reunites the two rings that they once exchanged in hope? Then you have a much more powerful scene, and a real impetus to join her.

Ann Liebeck, my first Lucia, was appalled when I told her.

'I don't *really* have to get into a coffin?' she wailed.

'I've tried it,' I said. 'It's exactly two minutes from when you climb in to when he takes the lid off.'

She shook her head.

I'd already had it built, and we had drilled ten holes in the shape of a cross above where her face would be. 'Look!' I said. 'It looks really cosy.'

She turned round and shuddered.

We talked about it a bit more. But I kept my best argument till last.

'Just think, Ann,' I said. 'Every other Lucia in the world gets carted off after the mad scene, leaving Edgardo to hog Act III all by himself. You will be the first Lucia ever to completely upstage him without having to sing a note!'

'Yes . . .' she said. 'I *see!*'

So she climbed in. A perfect fit. We gingerly put the lid down and carried her backwards and forwards with the leather thongs. They were too painful for the pall bearers, and were replaced with plaited hemp.

Suddenly everyone started laughing.

I turned round – six disembodied fingers were creeping out of the air holes and bending and clawing the air.

'Do that again,' said Kitty, when she opened the lid, 'and I'll leave you in there overnight!'

From then on, Ann made the most of her coffin and it had a strong dramatic effect. *But . . .* I couldn't face trying to get it on an aeroplane. So we sent Pico the specification, and this morning Ann and I went off to the Het Loo workshops to try out the one they have been making for me there. It is exact – beautifully made. The Dutch workmen were delighted to see her in it: lots of incomprehensible jokes and backslapping. They've done a fine job.

A rather disconcerting incident after the show. We had had to swap the bedrooms in the hotel around because of building noise. I was just closing my eyes when a note was pushed under my door.

'Can we continue our discussion? I am in the corridor.'

It was signed by one of the organizers of our tour. I stared at it, then glanced at my watch. One o'clock in the morning! Then I understood. The hotel register would list this room under the name of the girl who had moved to my quieter room. What should I do? Obviously he had made some headway. She might be expecting him. But if I came out, he might be hugely embarrassed, or else furious because it would appear that I had forestalled him. I could hear him pacing outside. I was too tired to face it, and went to sleep.

October 18

I told her about the note, and she protested that they had only discussed costume. She can sort it out if she wants to.

Chris Newell, tall and rangy, with a biblical beard, was our first producer. His *Così fan tutte* and *Don Pasquale* formed the bedrock of our early work. Now he is back. His production of *Fledermaus* is brilliant. It is completely idiosyncratic in so far as there is so much new ground, and yet it is all woven into an entirely believable period piece. I've seen six other productions of *Fledermaus*, all more or less good. But this is in a different league – especially Stefan's Frank, the prison governor, which has a Feydeau feel to the inspired characterization, quite unlike the dreary buffoons normally associated with this role. Tonight we did it at Amerongen, the sixteenth-century castle where the

Kaiser was interned at the end of the Great War and where he signed his abdication. The performance was at the top of the great stairs in a two-storey room hung with Bentincks and dominated by the Kaiser's white marble bust. One of the (interminable) opening speeches made the point that we were an English company performing in German a French play adapted by an Austrian composer, tonight before a Dutch audience. Truly *communautaire*.

They loved it – lots of laughs and a standing ovation. Reinier was sitting next to Marie-Lilian van Zoelen, who at one time was married to an Austrian Ambassador.

'Tell me,' he asked afterwards, 'did that bring back memories of Old Vienna?'

'No,' she said, after a pause. 'It was verry, verry English.'

October 20

Così at Het Huys Ten Donck, Pico's house, went really well last night. Enid's Dorabella was a triumph. Pico made a splendid speech about holidays and playboys and laid on caviare afterwards.

A quick look at the Rijksmuseum Vermeers, and we are now on the flight home, ready for Wardour tomorrow.

I can't really explain why I love opera so much. I don't suppose anyone can explain their passions. You love one woman, and are indifferent to another. It is the same with recreations.

My tutor at school used to play us *La Bohème*, and my father took me to Rossini's *Barber of Seville* in Rome when I was fifteen. I didn't much like either – I still don't. But I had become enthralled by Mozart's music, so I suppose I was halfway there. Then, when I was 18, I followed a girl I was in love with to Paris, and took her to see *Tannhäuser* and *Don Carlos* two nights running in the Palais Garnier, then as now the most beautiful opera house in the world.

And something happened. The girl? The setting? That Chagall ceiling? I don't know, though I do remember that Ticho Parly sang Tannhäuser, and Nicolai Ghiaurov sang King Philip. And since then I have been totally committed to opera: the drama, the music, the dance, the sheer exuberant power that it, and it alone, exercises over my emotions.

October 22

The Magic Flute at Wardour. I really look forward to Wardour. It's mainly because of our hosts, Laura and John Talbot. Every year they have us all to stay, they always give us a delicious supper, and then masses of sandwiches and wine afterwards as well. They're the last to go to bed (refusing all offers of help), and the first up to cook us all breakfast on our way west. But add to that the grandeur of Paine's façade, the wonderful approach through the remnants of Fonthill (especially William Kent's stupendous arch) and an invariably sympathetic audience, and the result is an especially happy evening.

I was so relaxed today that I lingered over lunch with my agent Gill Coleridge and didn't arrive until an hour before the show. I was just chatting to the Talbots when Kitty came up. She had her toothpaste smile in place, but the eyes were blazing.

'Did you know that Helen was singing Pamina?' she asked.

'Yes. Isn't it exciting?'

'Yes,' she hissed, smiling all the while. 'The costume has to be altered for her.'

'I'd completely forgotten. I'm very sorry.'

'That's all right, Freddie.'

She picked up a wooden chair and drove it so hard into the floor that all four legs snapped. Picking up the pieces, smiling her dreadful smile, she walked away.

The Talbots stared after her, thunderstruck. Well, I thought, if she can smile, so can I. I even managed a light laugh.

'We have to check the props to see if they're safe,' I explained. There was a long silence while the Talbots stared at me.

'But that was one of *our* chairs.'

October 23

So, down to work with *The Marriage of Figaro*. The first thing I do when preparing to direct an opera is to listen to the tapes in the car until I am saturated with the music. When I feel I know every phrase, I am already beginning to form mental pictures of how certain scenes might look, of the sort of expressions different characters might be assuming.

The most testing lesson I learnt when I first took over a production, at short notice due to the very abrupt departure of the original director, was that every gesture, every movement, of every singer, has to be planned. In the absence of specific direction, they are as likely as not to fall back on something they remember from a previous production, or indeed to stand still and expressionless until they receive further direction.

In that first hectic production we reached the dress rehearsal in four days and the hero, as he finished his first romantic aria, put his finger in his ear and rotated it slowly and with great intensity. Cor blimey, I thought, couldn't he have waited ten seconds until he'd gone off stage? I gave it no further thought. We dashed to Blickling in Norfolk, that masterpiece of Jacobean bravura, for the first night. On he came, belted out the aria and stuck his finger in his ear again. It was only then that I realized it must have been part of the original tasteless production. I hadn't spotted it, and thus it remained in his mental catalogue of gestures to be made.

I went upstairs to our dressing-room.

'Er . . . Philip?'

'Yes, Freddie?' He was all attention.
'I think we might cut the finger in the ear.'
'Right.'

Once familiar with the music, I then study the libretto, marking the phrases that I want to try to concentrate on for communicating to the audience. Alfred Hitchcock always planned his films on the basis that you should be able to follow the story without the sound-track, which he treated as a rich vein of extra embroidery. This formula is peculiarly appropriate for us, as we always sing in the original language. This used to be a great bone of contention with interviewers, who thought it both élitist and deliberately obscurantist. My explanation that music composed to fit one language could never fit so happily with another, and that opera sung in English is largely unintelligible anyway, fell on hostile ground. Perhaps I should have told the greater truth – that I loathe opera in English because translating the eighteenth century's taste for repetition usually makes something I love sound ridiculous – and anyway, with music, I like to be allowed to use my own imagination. In love scenes, as in horror movies, there is nothing so potent as the unknown.

The next step is to go back to the original sources. This not only helps to explain some of the librettist's intentions (what he has concentrated on, what he has deliberately omitted), but also sometimes provides suggestions for production detail. In this case I had studied both of Beaumarchais' plays, *The Barber of Seville* and *The Marriage of Figaro*, at school, so that it was a pleasure to re-read them. (Last year I struggled through their sequel, *La Mère Coupable*, to see if it was worth trying to commission a new score. No wonder there is no English translation on the market – the master had wholly lost his touch.)

Having now a clearly-framed picture of the whole opera, I then have to write the stage directions down on a doctored libretto (every other page a blank sheet of paper for the endless notes). This is like drawing before painting: skimped, there will be a pressing need for instant reactions in rehearsal; carefully done, it will sustain the progress of the production.

In theory. In practice, the success of an opera production depends entirely on the individual singers. Some can act, some cannot. Some will act for one director and not for another. But they are the raw material, and it is their skills that the director has to draw out and then encourage in the direction he thinks will best illustrate the story for the audience.

I am not a fan of the political-message school of direction, still less of the 'let's make *Magic Flute* seem specially relevant by setting it in a Little Chef' gang; they have roughed up too many favourite masterpieces. The common denominator of these two approaches is arrogance coupled with a contempt for the audience. The *Spectator* opera critic Rodney Milnes has written of the Royal Opera board having only 'superficial consumerist' values. And yet, what is opera for, if not to entertain the consumer, the audience? Certainly that is how Mozart and Verdi saw it – nor does that imply pandering to the lowest common denominator of taste. Great art sells better than pastiche. The same insidious self-importance has brought us tower blocks and other honours.

Thus to *Figaro*, an opera so full to overflowing with political and social messages as to make it an explosive property throughout Europe in the eighteenth century, and wholly absorbing two hundred years later. Several of the houses we perform in echo its plot to a startling degree, particularly in the context of social harmony.

At the start we are introduced to Susanna and Figaro, servants in a castle. It is their wedding-day, but Susanna is afraid that the Count, their master, has designs on her. Figaro boasts that he can outwit him. We meet some more characters: Dr Bartolo who bears Figaro a grudge, Marcellina who would like to marry Figaro, Cherubino a young page in love with his godmother the Countess, and Don Basilio whose job is to smooth the Count's path to Susanna's bed.

Next appear the Count, as amorous as we expected, and the Countess, depressed by his constant infidelities. These eight characters form and reform various alliances to battle out the complications of the day, which ends with Figaro married to Susanna, Marcellina married to Bartolo (now revealed as Figaro's long-lost parents!), and the Count and Countess reconciled. It's a splendid story full of *gaffes*, jealousy, confused identities, furious rows and reconciliations.

Because we perform in the round, naturalism is the basic ground rule. Don't over-act (a difficult hurdle for our recruits from some stage companies), but concentrate on the text. How would you look and feel in such a predicament? But above all – can you still sing beautifully while doing this? It is opera our audiences have paid for – so I don't demand arias on stepladders or tricycles.

The greatest compliment is if you can see the audience understanding the characters' emotions. If, because of some mannerism or a series of expressions, they can in a complex scene (I don't mean a happy character singing a happy aria, but perhaps a frightened woman trying to show confidence) say, 'Yes, I understand exactly how she's feeling', then we have succeeded.

The first question is how everyone is to look. We know we are just before the French Revolution, so there will be plenty of fashion books available. I don't like to see any trivialization of the Count and Countess – he is sometimes presented as a comically idiotic country squire. We're told he is the Governor of his province, and a grandee. Why ignore Beaumarchais? The threat of him reviving the 'droit de seigneur' makes less sense if he is insignificant.

The designer knows my penchant for bright colours and lavishly costumed footmen. His plans for the Countess are sumptuous. I'm going to go for an 'indoor' and an 'outdoor' look – pale, wan faces for the château's inhabitants, all of whom, masters and servants, are destined to be swept away by the

Revolution. Beaumarchais set the action of the play in Spain in order to conciliate French censorship protecting the Ancien Régime, so the outside servants, gardeners and so on, will have a rough, sunburnt colouring.

The mood? Talleyrand spoke nostalgically of the 'douceur de vivre' of pre-Revolutionary France, banished for ever by the guillotine. I don't think this meant only luxury. Look at the banter in the play:

> COUNT: 'Why does a servant in this house take longer to dress than his master?'
>
> FIGARO: 'Perhaps because he hasn't got his own valet?'

So – there will be all the signs of a prosperous, cheerful, rural household – sudden bursts of laughter, servants relaxing when alone, the normal courtesies between server and served, but with just a suggestion that the Count needs to be watched – he has an unpredictable temper. For the non-singing servants on stage, I am supremely fortunate in having two experienced members of the team – Colin, who is in charge of wardrobe, and Bruce Carter, who looks after lighting and acts as assistant stage manager. What they see as a minor part of their job, I see as a major contribution. As two footmen they have built up a marvellous range of thinly veiled expressions – exasperation, hard-boiled indifference, wild anticipation, discreet lust – I often can't take my eyes off them as they pass and repass – perfect examples of how different threads of life continue in a house or in a street, unaffected by the louder dramas that may hold the centre stage.

I *do* belong to the Expressionist–Pointillist School: by putting in infinitesimal details (which are more than likely to be overlooked by any average member of the audience), eventually I can build up an atmosphere which 'sets off' the opera. People may miss the detail, but they will be affected by the whole.

Here, because we're dealing with a complete day, the picture will be built up as follows:

6 a.m.   Count creeps back to room (?also Basilio)

7 a.m.	Logs and coal brought in	Overture
8 a.m.	Susanna supervises opening shutters	
9 a.m.	Breakfast on trays for Count and Countess	
10 a.m.	A clock strikes	(in between Act 1 and 2)
11 a.m.	Countess has a cup of chocolate	
1 p.m.	Lunch gong	(end of Act 2)
3 p.m.	Count is feeling sleepy	
5 p.m.	Sun begins to glow orange	
6 p.m.	Count served with a drink	
7 p.m.	Supper	(end of Act 3)
8 p.m.	Twilight and shadows	
Midnight	Everyone distinctly ready for bed	(end of Act 4)

The next step is to define the main characters.

Figaro must be active, bright and full of ideas ('un vesuvio' he describes himself in Rossini's *Barber*). But one of the enjoyable effects of *The Marriage* is that all his stratagems fail – he is always found out (by the Count, by Antonio, by Susanna), whereas Susanna (Beaumarchais demands that she be dressed in white, presumably to underline her virginity) always succeeds, whether in raising her dowry (borrowed from the Countess) or in making fools of the Count and Figaro (Act 4).

The Count is obviously imperious, lustful and dangerous. But he has a nice line in irony, and takes Figaro's increasing lack of respect in his stride. Since he is pursuing both Susanna and her cousin Barbarina simultaneously we may assume that he is unhappy, and he is so easily disconcerted at the end that he must have a generous nature. The Countess is more complex. She proclaims constant despair at losing her husband's love (starting in the same key as Mozart's audience would previously have heard her as Rosina in Paisiello's preceding *Barber*), and yet she is obviously affected by her little page's attentions (so much so, indeed, that she has a child by him three years later). The play has much more on this than the opera libretto, so I intend to build on that. Marcellina is usually played for laughs, yet she has the most beautiful aria in the opera (if I can find anyone able to sing it). The funniest scene (Figaro's discovery that his two enemies are his parents) might work even better if we can build in some pathos. It would, after all, be a shattering experience. The story has, like all great comedies, a fair element of sadness. Infidelity is usually only funny if you are not concerned in it yourself.

Provisional casting will be:

Figaro	Noel
Susanna	Helen
Countess Almavira	Alice
Basilio	Blair (*understudied by Peter*)
Curzio	Bruce (*a small role which he will enjoy for a change*)
Cherubino	Enid
Barbarina	Susan (*understudied by Amy*)

The main gap is the Count. But more auditions are looming, so I must wait and hope.

October 25

Generally I have concentrated on the voices and features of the singers, largely because these are the characteristics most apparent to the audiences who keep us in business. But there are other qualities that matter – like niceness. Arthur Coomber, next year's Rigoletto, is one of the nicest men I have ever met. Kindly, modest, unassuming, remorseless in driving himself forward in his work yet invariably patient with others, he sets a very high standard of conduct for the rest of us. The day he won the heart of the prettiest girl in the company was one of universal celebration.

I only discovered yesterday that he moonlights as a jeweller when not plotting murder for me. Many professional singers cultivate secondary careers – just in case: Noel is a percussionist, Colin makes ball dresses, Bryan teaches the piano to a select and lucky few, Bruce Rankin has taught English, and Alan Fairs A-level Economics.

I set my alarm early this morning because there was a message on my answering machine to say that the *Independent* review of *Lucia* would be published today. I pulled some old trousers over my pyjamas, grabbed an overcoat and walked to the corner shop. The journey was worthwhile.

Pavilion Opera's home is Thorpe Tilney Hall, near Lincoln, but you are most likely to encounter this exciting young company in the galleries and reception rooms of country houses up and down the land. Give them a candle-lit room, a square of carpet, and a grand piano and they will provide in return a musically vibrant, richly-costumed, original language performance of one of the surprisingly large repertoire of operas they tour each year.

This season, which Sotheby's are sponsoring, there are six operas on the road, including new productions of *Die Fledermaus*, *Il Barbiere*, and *Lucia di Lammermoor*, which played last Saturday evening a mile or two west of Reading in the Long Gallery of Englefield House, a stately pile that even away from gloomy Scottish glens has all the moody Gothic atmosphere you need for Donizetti's setting of Scott's tragic tale.

Played in such a context, the work took on a new and terrifying immediacy. At Covent Garden we sit in a gilded barn of a theatre. Here, though, we were in a private house, and Englefield might for all the world have been Ravenswood in the 1690s. As clocks chimed down nearby corridors and dogs barked in the park to the sound of Lucia's own demented bayings, we were witnessing a political and domestic tragedy of an immediacy that even Puccini might have envied.

The evening could have been said to have started inauspiciously when Pavilion's energetic pianist and music director, Bryan Evans, launched into a Palm Court rendition of the great Act Two sextet. But after that there were no let-ups. What we were given was a full-blooded performance of the traditional text sung and acted with unbridled commitment by this talented group of artists.

The audience had turned out to hear Donizetti and support a new ecumenical church in far-away Milton Keynes (Pavilion performances are often tied in to charitable ventures), but they also had a lesson in the lung power of professional singers. Once or twice the Edgardo, Bruce Rankin, seemed to be ignoring pianissimo opportunities as a matter of policy, though he sang more inwardly and with great intensity in the opera's closing scene. Elsewhere, the singing was stylish and direct.

There were strong performances of Raimondo and Arturo by Noel Mann and Timothy Evans-Jones and outstanding portrayals of Lucia and the all-powerful Enrico by Ann Liebeck, a coloratura song-bird of great youthful promise, and George Mosley. Mosley's singing was especially cultured, and his acting was a model of astuteness and simplicity.

It is a style that the company seems to have down to a fine art. Blair Wilson's Normanno was played with an energy and watchfulness that *comprimarios* playing in bigger houses rarely attempt. No wonder some people thought this the most vivid *Lucia* they had ever seen.

It may not sell tickets, but it's a great boost to our morale, individual and collective.

October 26

At tea today our employers brought in some bottles of hock. The cast looked pleased, but for me this brought back hideous memories of *Don Pasquale* at Heath Mount School. The Don Pasquale of the day had a fearful cold and was otherwise depressed as well. In one of the intervals, the Headmaster had generously placed a bottle of whisky in the dressing room for the cast to share after the show.

The first half had gone well, and I had no worries. The patter duet seemed a bit garbled but perhaps no more than usual. We got through the garden scene, and in came Don Pasquale to uncover the plot, ready for the final quartet. It's a character part, intended for caricature, but this time he seemed especially out of control. Weaving this way and that, leering at the audience, grumbling under his breath . . . it was quite a performance. I still had no premonition. Then suddenly, with a thunderous crash, he fell over behind my grandmother's *chaise longue*. Absolute silence. I waited for him to get up – nothing happened. Suddenly I realized Bryan was playing on without him.

'What . . . ?'

'He's drunk!' he whispered.

'WHAT??'

Ernesto was gaping at us: Norina had a face of fury. Dr Malatesta saved the day by improvising the bass line, and then they swept into the quartet (now a trio). The audience seemed impressed by the old man's sudden end, and clapped the others with enthusiasm as they carried him out. So, no apologies today as I pick up the wine bottles and carry them out, watched by a number of angry faces. Too bad. There's time enough to drink after the show.

October 27

A dreary performance to a dreary audience. No icon is so lovingly varnished, none so furiously guarded, as one's image of oneself. As Burns has it,

> O wad some pow'r the giftie gie us
> To see oursels as others see us!

Well, thanks very much. Hooray for Burns. Facing the mirror before breakfast is more than enough for me. But today I had to acknowledge that I do have a very bad temper. I don't know what sets it off. Most of the time I like to think that I am the most slavishly good-natured appeaser. 'Yes, Nanny.' 'Yes, darling.' 'Yes, Bryan.' As the warlords in my life thunder hither and thither commanding my allegiance, I am really happy to acquiesce. But today, a bore of bores tried me too far. I shouted at him at lunchtime. When he approached me in the interval I shouted at his attempt to smile. I've felt ill with rage all day, and it's done no one any good. Oh yes, I know what sets it off. Malignant incompetence, a rare but explosively infuriating form of malice. But Bruce and Susan sang superbly.

October 28

Another personal failing is instant susceptibility. What is that fatal magic that sparks off the exhilaration and agony of affection?

Tonight, in Yorkshire, we had one of our nervous employers. Supremely confident up to the moment we arrived, one look at us and he was thrown into the pit of despair. The performance was going to be abysmal. He would be humiliated. Luckily he had a middle-aged couple from Worcestershire staying, George and Jane Holinshed, friends of my late sister, who bolstered him up and actually got him out of the house while we set up.

During the performance Jane Holinshed sat in the front row. How can I describe her? Glossy black hair, she had dressed simply, in a way that enhanced her opulence rather than distracted the attention. There was a triangular line to her forearm, she had very pale blue eyes and a creamy complexion shot with scarlet. She blushed when she laughed, an even richer scarlet that highlighted her cheekbones, and when she smiled at Bryan and me, I felt suddenly cold. What is that magic? I think it is expression – the expression on a face that after thirty years reveals more of the character than youthful prettiness ever can.

That night I thought of Bernstein in *Citizen Kane*.

'One day (back in 1896),' he said, 'I was crossing on a ferry and there was a girl on another ferry, waiting to get off. She was carrying a white parasol – I only saw her for one second. But I'll bet a month hasn't gone by that I haven't thought of that girl.'

And, again, of Stanley Holloway paraphrasing Whittier in *The Lavender Hill Mob*: 'Of all sad words of tongue and pen, the saddest are these: "It might have been".'

I've always wondered if he knew the parody:

> If of all sad words of tongue and pen
> The saddest are 'it might have been'
> Sadder are these we daily see:
> 'It is but hadn't ought to be!'

Don Pasquale's curtain call.

October 30

Tonight I had Valentine, my youngest son, with me. Like the other two, Harry and Alexander, he is remarkably patient with his father. I think it does help that they know the singers well, and all play the piano – an odd omission from the core curriculum, since it promotes co-ordination and a sense of rhythm.

He sits beside me, sometimes drumming his legs but leaning forwards, head thrust out, watching the action. Just before the last act, he suddenly walks out. Panic! Does he hate it? Is he cross that his rare and precious time away from school is hijacked into this complicated arena of alternative, even fiercer, discipline? We wait, Bryan tense because the singers may not realize that their cue is delayed. No – here he comes.

'Where have you *been*?' I hiss.

'I was bursting,' he whispers back. I *do* understand! And now we're off into the finale. I think he really does enjoy it. I hope so, because I love having him with me.

November 1

The golden rule in opera is that anything that can go wrong, will. Skirts rip, swords snap, chairs collapse. And the audience love it – while the rest of us panic. Tonight we did *Traviata* with the (new) producer in the audience. The way he's set it, the lights dim and Violetta comes in in her nightdress, eerily looking around the room as if searching for the ghosts of her past. The whole of the rest of the cast are huddled outside, ready to enter as the music changes to re-create the first of Flora's parties. So . . . in she came: the producer was intent to see how his production was received. The audience fell silent. But before Violetta had even crossed the room a large county lady, in tweeds, sprang to her feet, pushed past her and ran to the double doors. What? Leaving already? Now, I know these doors. Carefully handled they work fine – but they can stick. She grabbed both handles, and twisted them the wrong way. Nothing happened. Violetta had a glassy look, but was carrying on slowly. Uppermost in her mind and mine was that the only way into the room was now jammed. Behind the door was a whole heap of people desperate to get in. What was worse, it was the only way out. We were trapped. The woman was still fiddling with the doors. She then turned for help to the nearest person – the producer, who by this time was giving her a death-wish stare of unparalleled ferocity. If looks had any practical effect, she would have burst into flames. I could see the handle being frantically twisted from the other side. Violetta's eyes were in shock. And then the producer, suppressing a snarl, rose, crossed to the doors, kicked one sharply and opened the other. Helen and the others fell into the room, and the woman turned round and walked back to her seat!

In the interval, I found her.

'Do tell me. Why did you try to leave?' I asked.

'Oh, it was only that I thought I was going to cough. I was afraid it might put the singers off.'

November 2

Up early to collect some more programmes from the Pavilion *en route* for Sledmere. The Humber Bridge saves about an hour on this journey, so it suits us, if no one else. While some houses seem perpetually haunted by glowering troglodytes, Sledmere has always had the great fortune to be filled with luminous characters. Arthur Syegrove, Mrs Marshall, Mr Healey and Dorothy may live only in affectionate memory, but Michael, Jack, Maureen and Mrs Hines smile on to encourage the grateful visitor. But what has happened to Tony? Asked to switch on my bedroom fire during a New Year visit, he contemptuously flung open the window onto the frosty morning, and flounced out of the room with an angry snort!

The house was always welcoming, despite – or perhaps because of – the overpowering character of Tatton Sykes' father, the celebrated 'Mutant'. For fifty years he presided over it as it was transformed from a fine country house encompassed by its thirty-six thousand acres, into a glittering palazzo anxiously supported by a narrowing ribbon of landscaped wolds. With his death, the fear that deliciously haunted every doorway has abated, but the memory lingers. To give some idea of his pervasive power: you might be lying in your bath, safe on the top floor behind a locked door. Suddenly, the water would shiver and ripple, the whole room begin to vibrate. And you would know. It was the 'Mutant', thundering away at the organ – a sort of country-house Vincent Price with the added horror of

"No – I think it's
the Mutant playing
Bach"

being real, for those distant reverberations were an immediate reminder of the threat of his sudden and unpredictable rages. Whole house parties would be packed off at a moment's notice, furniture thrown out of the window (never his own) – no, it's all over. They buried him more than ten years ago; but, as I say, the memory remains.

November 3

Lunched with Perry St John. He is on one of his usual imperceptible diets. This time it's one meal a day – by mischance, the very one to which he had asked himself. He ordered three main courses, which he ate with such gusto that his green Hermès tie was speckled with oil by the end. I offered him half a bottle of Chablis (since I was drinking water). 'Do you know?' he said, 'I've taken to having a whole bottle, even if I don't drink it all. Do you ever find yourself doing that?' 'Not often,' I replied, without adding '– at least, not when I'm a guest.' A hugely fat man came in, his shirt and trousers positively erupting with ill-contained flesh. 'That's the sort of person one wants to have around when one's dieting,' I suggested, but Perry wouldn't even look at him.

Blair rang tonight. He wants a few days off to visit an aunt in Philadelphia. I rang Bruce, who was willing to take over. It leaves us exposed without an understudy, but I think we can take the risk.

November 4

Glemham in Suffolk is such a beautiful house, Elizabethan with some Georgian refacing. Our employer, Lady Blanche Cobbold, was in Canada with the Athlones during the Great War, and had lots of anecdotes. I was the first to arrive, and she had laid out tea, with the help of a very drunk cook.

'PUT ANOTHER LOG ON THAT FIRE!' Her commanding voice echoed in the hall as I came downstairs, to find her gesticulating at Dr Malatesta. He had just arrived to ask if this was the right house. I thought I had better intervene.

'Let me do it.' He has a notoriously short fuse, but some form of wonderful rapport had been established. Not only did he patiently build up the fire, but he even helped with the washing-up after the cook, by now incapable, had been helped to her room after dinner.

No problem with the performance, but that night the house was bitterly cold. I had been warned already – 'It's very simple, just put the carpet on your bed.' Easier said than done, in my case, since there was only linoleum. I was just wondering if my carpet had been looted by Bryan next door, when someone tapped. I opened my door to find three gleaming sopranos in their nightdresses. Aha! This was what being an impresario is all about! But no, all they wanted to find out was whether it was safe to go downstairs to fill their hot-water bottles.

Thanks to Bryan, I'm off tomorrow to Russia. The Ambassador has fixed up a possible booking next year subject to the room being suitable.

November 5

The British Embassy, Moscow. My bedroom window in this huge cream palace faces directly across the Moscow River to the Kremlin's floodlit Baroque façade which was built for Alexander II after the defeat of Napoleon, but in the style of a hundred years earlier, and is massively impressive.

My first sight of Russia was *wonderful* – we came hurtling down through thick rolling clouds into a satanic gloom and then, suddenly, glimpses of vast dark forests covered in snow that vanished and then loomed up at us in the eerie fog. Not a sign of human existence – just miles and miles of forest that might have been sold to pay for Natasha's rubies, or for a ball on her name-day.

Reality – that the people are starved and subjugated by fear of a tiny minority of unsmiling fanatics. But then, Russia has always been ruled by force since Peter the Great succeeded in dragging the princes into one state. It is extraordinary to think that most of the countries we know – Germany, Italy, Belgium, Holland, Austria, for example, are less than one hundred and fifty years old. Even Barclays Bank is older. Russia may be two hundred and seventy-five, but we forget how suddenly things change. Yet all that they have done is to swap one oligarchy for another.

Anyway, it was fun being collected in a Rolls flying the Union Jack, and it looks as if we shall be performing *Figaro*. Certainly the room is perfect – all white and gold, with four sets of double doors and every surface covered in moulded plaster decoration. Conversation at dinner with Rodric and Gill Braithwaite covered Islam, Homer, the siege of Vienna and whether Pauline Viardot ever slept with Turgenev. There is a chance that they will get me a ticket for Tchaikovsky's *Queen of Spades* at the Bolshoi tomorrow.

November 6

The choice of opera is rarely controversial. Sometimes the client is certain. '*Traviata* is my favourite opera. That's the one we want.'

No problems there, at least not my end.

Sometimes they are delightfully constructive: 'Which opera do *you* think would work best?' Then we look at the room, the entrances, the style of audience, the overall feel of the house, and decide accordingly.

A balcony suggests *Barber* or *Rigoletto*, three or four doors open up possibilities for *Figaro* or *Hoffmann*, a church is right for *Magic Flute*, a barn for *Elisir d'amore*, and a staircase for *Traviata*, *Merry Widow* or *Lucia*. Musical groups favour Mozart, private parties are impatient of German dialogue, heavy architecture is best complemented by grand tragedy.

My main perk is being able to decide on the repertoire. I have two main criteria – I have to be able to enjoy each opera two or three times a week for a whole year, and to believe in it so that I can truthfully encourage any employer to be confident of its selling potential.

For me, operas fall into four categories – accessible masterpieces, inaccessible masterpieces, one-aria works, and duds. Examples of the first are *Figaro* and *Traviata*, of the second *Rheingold* and *Lulu*, of the third *Nabucco* and *Suor Angelica*, and of the fourth and wholly subjectively, absolutely everything ever written by Benjamin Britten.

We stick obstinately to the first category – and since ninety per cent of our work is with piano, naturally I choose the pieces that will work best in this way. *Rigoletto*, not *Otello*; *Tosca*, not *Butterfly*. How do I know, I who cannot read music? Because Bryan is beside me, and he does know. I managed to talk him into *Lucia*. I am still trying with *Norma* and *Fidelio*.

Finally, there is one more hurdle. Is the story sufficiently strong to benefit from our very detailed style of presentation? Operas of great musical delight but ludicrously idiotic storyline fall at this last fence: Flotow's *Martha*, Donizetti's *Fille du Régiment*, Mozart's *Clemenza di Tito* – all good stuff, but best left to the recording studios.

We have definitely agreed on *Figaro*.

The Ambassador's secretary, who speaks fluent Russian, was given the task of amusing me. We walked to the Kremlin (minus ten degrees and drifting snowflakes). Across the river and in through one of the massive brick towers of the encircling fifteenth-century brick walls. It is very high, with colossal towers, the saddest one named 'the maiden' because it has never been breached (poor thing). The Kremlin itself has a series of dramatic cathedrals with newly gilded domes – each cathedral has at least five (the large central one for God the Father and then the four Apostles), but some have as many as nineteen. It was curious to see the tombs of Ivan the Terrible and his family, even those mentioned in *Boris Godunov*; most poignantly that of little Prince Dmitri.

Back through Red Square and across the river and into the warm panelled Embassy for half a pint of vodka to restore the circulation, then – no delay – off with a new driver through the crowded streets at break-neck speed. (There is a special diplomatic lane, like the bus lane in London, symbolic of the difference between a people's republic – top people only – and a capitalist state – public transport only.) We drove straight across the pedestrian precinct scattering the docile masses, who in London would have turned the car over and set it on fire. But when we reached the theatre for *The Queen of Spades*, we had to clamber over a mass of scaffolding. The theatre itself (1856) is as in Tsarist days, except that the Royal Box now sports a Hammer and Sickle instead of the Imperial Eagle. The orchestra played well, but the acting and direction were astoundingly bad. The seventeen-year-old heroine, object of several men's helpless devotion, looked and behaved like a prize sow. She was so fat that she couldn't move her head at all, and her eyes were lost in a Uralian range of blubber. The hero was so camp and over the top in his acting that her greatest triumph was in not laughing when, for example, he leapt three feet in the air and entwined himself on a chair (with his feet over one arm) to signify his fright at a clock striking at night. Knowing the story, I understood. Many others must have been mystified, particularly as the clock missed its cue and remained silent during this drama, striking rather half-heartedly after the story had moved on. But the ballet in Act 2 was beautiful, and in great contrast to the leaden singers.

November 7

A quick expedition this morning before my flight home, to visit Khrushchev's grave. I would rather have rested, but it seemed ungrateful to my hostess, so off we set and got lost in the suburbs, exciting considerable interest with our flag. But it was all very worthwhile because the silver-and-green-domed monastery turned out to be the setting for *Boris Godunov* Act 1, Scene 1 – where he is persuaded to proclaim himself Tsar, having strangled the little boy whose tomb I saw yesterday.

November 8

More auditions, and what is more, the perfect Count Almaviva (and, indeed, Don Giovanni), *and* the perfect Commendatore, on the same day. No problem with the latter, Alan Fairs, who has been working at Glyndebourne; but the former, Roberto Salvatori from Trinidad, has no work permit. But he is excellent, so I must try.

Why do singers queue to join us? It certainly isn't the money! Although we pay well compared to other small subsidized groups like D'Oyly Carte and Opera 80, the major companies have the advantage of huge subsidies levied from you and me by the Inland Revenue, and naturally they can pass this on to their artists. At the beginning it was straightforward – our season was only a couple of months. If you had no other work and if we were at least paying the Union minimum, why not? But now that our season runs for ten months, negotiated a year in advance, it is a considerable commitment, and cuts you off from other potential employment.

Ours are all Principal singers, the generic term used to identify those who are committed to singing principal roles rather than earning an easy living from chorus and session work. Taken overall, they probably earn less because of the large proportion who fail to reach the pinnacles for which they have slaved, practising at home and learning roles, while their easy-going contemporaries pick up regular pay cheques by mouthing at the back of well-known stages.

To give a simple example, there are probably forty good Susannas aged between 25 and 40 available in Britain. There will be one at Covent Garden, one at English National Opera, one with Scottish and a fourth with Welsh. Glyndebourne and Opera North may have imported theirs. Others will have found employment overseas, usually in Germany, and another half-dozen are having babies. That leaves twenty for us to choose from, although two or three of these will prefer a tiny role (Barbarina, say) at Covent Garden to a major role with me. The good news is that each casting panel has different criteria. I wouldn't have swapped Helen Kucharek for any of her competitors – and it was nice to read that the *Independent* agreed. She has a sparkling stage presence and a voice of ethereal beauty; after the show, the dressing room is besieged by nervous admirers.

I believe, therefore, that the reason singers want to join us is to gain the experience of performing major roles ten years earlier than they could expect to get the parts in the big houses, where the gloomy rule of 'dead men's shoes' so often preponderates. As long as they have a Rosalinde in her fifties or even sixties, the aspiring forty-year-olds will grow grey waiting for the part. And so on. The age at which Johann Strauss envisaged the role would be cast is the late twenties – and the Rosalindes of that age are available for me! Long may it continue, I say, so long as I don't have to attend those prehistoric obsequies.

November 9

Packing up for Algeria. Lots of complaints about injections. I have agreed to pay for hepatitis and cholera out of the long-exhausted contingency reserve.

I have never met Philippa and Bridget, angels on the other end of the telephone at Montpellier Travel. Each year they juggle and struggle with our endlessly changing travel plans, trying to get us the best deals available. Until yesterday, we were routed via Frankfurt, but today came the good news that we have been squeezed onto a direct flight.

November 11

Algiers airport was chaos. Unruly mobs of young Arab men, jostling, shouting, not many smiles. We were lucky to be met by the Ambassador, Patrick Eyers, and helped through.

Dinner last night was a banquet, just for us and Patrick and Heidi Eyers' Belgian friend Madame Poirot, and served by Achmed, their Arab butler, in scarlet with a pointed, grizzled beard. Whose body, I wondered, looking round at the various characters, would be found stretched out in the Library next morning, skewered by the scimitar above the door?

The most interesting sight this afternoon, out of a day spent visiting Roman ruins and viaducts, was the vast beehive tomb of Cleopatra's daughter by Mark Anthony, who married Juba,

King of Mauretania. I paced it out – it is almost exactly the dimensions (and indeed the shape) of the Albert Hall, poised massively within sight of the Atlas Mountains to the south, and of her beloved Mediterranean to the north.

The greatest drama so far has been a soprano's top A shriek when she opened one eye to see an immense rat, watching her sunbathing by the pool. Despite continuous horns, screeches, humming, from the city below, it's surprisingly restful. Madame Poirot is knitting something pink and small. In five minutes I shall have to meet the piano tuner.

November 12

A day to recover, and to go to church. We have quite a strong church-going group, including me. Today we went with Patrick and Heidi to the little Christian chapel. It was an odd feeling, perched on the northern tip of a gigantic continent mostly dedicated to other, more warlike gods. Blair has been going on at me for some time to let him try to teach me to sing.

'It's no good, Blair,' I would say. 'I just can't sing in tune.'

'Everyone can sing, Freddie. You let me hear you. I know you can do it.'

Well, today there were favourable circumstances. Blair was immediately in front of me. There was a good congregation to provide covering fire, and best of all, three favourite hymns: 238, 555 and 196, so . . . I took a deep breath and let rip:

> As pants the hart for cooling streams,
> When heated in the chase,
> So longs my soul, O God, for thee
> And Thy refreshing grace.

There was slight restlessness around me, but I paid no attention. It's a short hymn and we were soon into the General Confession, that sweet solace to the sore-hearted. None of the obscure mateyness of the Alternative Service in Algeria, I noted: just the familiar, comforting words of our traditional Prayer Book. Then the next hymn:

> Lord, enthroned in heavenly splendour
> First-begotten from the dead,
> Thou alone, our strong Defender,
> Liftest up Thy people's head.
> Alleluia! [deep breath] ALLELUIA!!
> Jesu, true and living Bread! [ga-a-asp]

The First Secretary, who was taking the service, cast a rather curious eye in our direction. But in for a penny, in for a pound. I saved my strongest effort for the final throw:

> Guide me, O Thou great Redeemer,
> Pilgrim through this barren land.

Hardened veterans of this hymn, the graveyard of many an ill-prepared congregation, know that one's greatest cunning must be reserved for the double crescendo of the penultimate line. My solution is to ignore the first round and then stun my exhausted neighbours with the strength of my contribution to the second:

> Feed me now and evermore, EVERMORE!
> Feed me now-ow-ow, and evermore!

I gave it my best shot. Blair's shoulders seemed to freeze. We polished off the second verse:

" As pants the hert... "

Be Thou still my strength and shield, STRENGTH AND SHIELD!
Be Thou stil-i-ill my-y strength and shield.

Phyllida turned and fixed me with a sympathetic look of deep
concern. I got the message and enjoyed the last verse in silence.
Blair left without a word.

November 13

Così went very well, apart from a nasty moment when Despina,
faced with the two disguised Albanians, went twirling round the
room exclaiming 'Che mustacchi! They might be Turks!!' I was
facing the Turkish Ambassador – others looked at him. I'd
completely forgotten – would he walk out? Perhaps he doesn't
understand Italian? No – he's smiling. At dinner I made some
sort of apology – quite unnecessary, as he knew the opera
intimately and saw no reason for offence. Jean the cook from
Kinshasa had had the job of keeping the servants quiet. He said
there was no problem as they were all listening at the doors. As
for him, he hid under the dining-room table opposite the
entrance, loving every minute, especially the quick costume
changes.

Most of the audience were diplomats or ministers. But one
was a beautiful girl whose legs had been blown off during the
war of secession from France. Another, even prettier, had lost
her husband, the then Foreign Minister, shot down while he was
trying to mediate between Iraq and Iran.

I'm supposed to be writing a synopsis of *Faust* but escaped to
visit the Casbah instead. It's a warren of ninth- to thirteenth-
century houses crammed together on a hill above the new city,
intersected only by tiny spiralling stone steps. Shouting,
laughing children, grim expressionless men, and scarcely a
woman in sight. The houses are completely plain outside but
with cool courtyards inside, with fountains and two or three

storeys of balustraded stuccoed Turkish arcades. Why? To keep the women out of sight.

Blair has studiously avoided reopening the subject of my voice . . .

November 20

From one extreme to another. We reached Geneva this evening having met at Heathrow to be filmed by the Swiss TV crew who had flown over to accompany our flight. They were intrigued by the idea of an opera company setting up shop in other people's châteaux.

'I see,' said their glamorous presenter. 'They are your family.'

This as the cast of *Così fan tutte* assembled. I pointed out that I had three wonderful sons – sufficient for any father.

She stared at me.

'You are a father?' What an insult. But I mentally watched myself to see if I had started mincing about or flapping my hands unnecessarily.

The cast were treated, and therefore behaved and dressed, like film stars. Alice, our blonde Texan Fiordiligi, had a black fur muff, scarlet lipstick and a long crocodile skin coat under a fur wrap.

'Why, Fred-deee! How're yuh, doll?' She was also wearing vast dark glasses. The camera crew scurried round to record my muttered response.

The other passengers were justifiably put out. Everything was filmed – singers eating, singers sleeping, an angry stewardess, an apoplectic steward. I hope it's worthwhile.

November 21

Although there's snow on the ground, we're performing in a crimson Indian tent attached to the château. There are practically more men in white coats, pushing champagne and caviare, than there are guests. The whole afternoon, I watched an army of contractors transplanting flowers in the garden. I also watched the light fading, so that now, as the guests arrive, you can't see a flower, or anything else.

I've had a stove moved next to the piano, but it's still very cold for Bryan to play.

Most of the afternoon I sat in a salon, reading Trollope while the singers were taken on a boat trip round Lake Geneva. Two colossal security men kept coming in and out, whispering into walkie-talkies and looking tremendously tough. This proved a sham. Suddenly, who knows why, there was a terrific clatter behind them as a plate fell off the wall and smashed on the floor. They both leapt in the air and ran off with the pieces to my employer. Later he came in, with a gloomy look.

'Disaster!' he said.

'It wasn't their fault. It just fell off the wall.'

'No, no. Not the plate. I've just heard that the *foie gras* has been held up at the border.'

This was bad news indeed. His wife had told me all about the *foie gras* at lunch.

The bell has just been rung. I shall have to abandon the Cathedral Close until later.

November 22

Not a great first act. The audience were the WORST EVER, totally silent. No smiles, no applause, nothing. They must *hate* it, I thought. Our first total flop. In the interval I saw Monique, who had organized the whole trip.

58

'Oh dear,' I said. 'It doesn't seem to be very popular.'

'But they're frrrrrozen. Simply frrrrrozen.' She was wrapped in fur.

It was true. As soon as I came away from the piano and our heater, it was obvious that the audience, in their décolletages, were chilled almost beyond the power of speech.

More stoves were brought, whisky distributed and the second half went differently. Even Switzerland's loveliest television presenter (who had had to stand outside interviewing guests as they came and went) had thawed.

But in the morning, the flowers were black.

November 23

Never try to be too clever. There's a motto for all of us. Delicious supper tonight with an old friend, Miles Jebb, after getting *Traviata* started at Gray's Inn. I was put next to a rather snooty young woman connected with Glyndebourne.

'I believe you do a little opera thing,' she said, without looking at me. I could hardly deny it.

'Excerpts? That sort of thing?' she pursued.

'No, we do try to soldier on to the end.' Frankly, I was more interested in the pâté. Couldn't we talk about gardening? I was quite willing to acknowledge her ascendancy in music.

'When was your last show?'

'Well, we're actually doing *Traviata* at the moment.'

'TRAVIATA?' There was so much ridicule in this that I felt sorely tried.

'How on earth do you manage to do that with a piano?' She made it sound like a tambourine.

'Well, you'd be surprised.' I decided to take her seriously and explain how it worked. It was all wasted effort.

'And so, you see,' I babbled on, 'the original story at Flora's party had only four people there, however many Zeffirelli may

use to fill up space. Verdi only wrote five singing lines in the
chorus music, so with twelve we are covering it quite well.
And', I added, developing my pet theme, 'we've done it rather
in the spirit of Swann and the Jockey Club. I'm really pleased
with it.'

'Swan?' she said, looking at me for the first and last time.
'Swan? I think you are getting confused with *Lohengrin*!' And
with that she turned her back.

November 24

Don Giovanni is much harder to cast than *Figaro*. The Don
himself must be plausible – that is, physically attractive, and
dangerous. There are various approaches to the work – some see
it as a comedy of constant failure, but I prefer to see it simply as
an adventure, the last chapters of a splendid villain's escapades.
The key to his relationship with Donna Anna lies in her *recitative*
with Don Ottavio, her fiancé, when he finally confronts her and
asks what happened before her father's murder by Don
Giovanni. The words (and in Mozart's operas, who knows who
wrote what? – though we know he was firm in changing
anything to suit his final design) can bear two interpretations.

'I thought it was you. Then I struggled. I screamed. I broke
free.'

I prefer the racier reading. Donna Anna must be as strong and
as imperious as her music, but she must also be sensual. We shall
need three Donna Annas because it is such a demanding part.
Caroline and Helen have already agreed. But I need one more in
case it is booked often.

Donna Elvira, the desecrated nun or avenging wife, depending
on which source you follow, is strident but easily deceived. She
is always ready to forgive the Don, obviously because she still
loves him. Zerlina the peasant girl, who in previous centuries

was seen as the prima donna of the show but who nowadays is more often undercast, is a great survivor. Bryan wants to cast her as a mezzo to improve the ensembles. This suggests Enid, covered perhaps by Anne her fellow New Zealander, for a suitably saucy interpretation.

Leporello, the Don's servant, will be Noel – and I shall hope to build a Holmes-and-Watson partnership between him and the Don: good fellowship one minute, anger the next, but inextricably bound together because of the escapades they have shared.

Masetto, Zerlina's fiancé, is really a non-part, but what of Don Ottavio? He has two of the world's most moving arias (admittedly, not originally intended to be performed both on the same night). Mozart was a master of musical characterization, and did not allocate beautiful music to a nonentity: and yet, Ottavio is so feeble, with nothing useful to say except as commanded by Donna Anna. Where Mozart did add in an aria just to help cast the part (Basilio in *Figaro*, Act 4) the result was not a success. So he must have intended these to tell us about Ottavio. Generous sentiments, slightly cloying, but beautifully presented – OK, he'll have to be nice, timid and a bit simple.

Add the usual ingredients of the Don's resplendent servants and a small stage band in the same livery, and I think it will work, given the designer Christopher Cowell's gift for strong colours in the costumes. I am absolutely fed up with *Don Giovanni* productions in black and grey and off-white. It's a brilliant piece, full of fire and passion. So I shall ask for scarlet, and gold, and blue, and then more gold. And, just as the primary colours will form pools of contrast on stage, so the production will have its moments of terror and of farce – moving from one to the other as quickly as possible. Who knows what is original, and what comes from the half-heard, half-picked up information from the past? Wherever it comes from, it seems valid to say that in *Figaro* all the women say no, so it's a comedy, whereas in *Don Giovanni* all the woman say yes, so it's a tragedy. Is this valid in real life? Let's hope not.

Provisional casting:

Don Giovanni	Roberto (*if I can get his work permit*)
Leporello	Noel
Donna Anna	Helen
Donna Elvira	shared between Alice and Susan
Zerlina	Enid
Masetto	Philip
Commendatore	the wonderful Alan Fairs

A strong cast for any company.

November 26

Back at Gooseleigh, that strangely dull mass of misplaced masonry in the West Midlands, and straight into trouble. Anne ffolliott is delightful and a very fine sculptress; Percy, however, is a more complicated character. I think I'm right to tell my potential employers next year's fees in advance so that no one books me in ignorance of the cost. Indeed, my view is that if people know the price, there is no need for complaint. You choose to buy, or not. But not Squire ffolliott, who gave me half an hour on the cost of culture.

Having had enough, I returned to London after the performance of *Fledermaus*, in the knowledge that we need never meet again; but alas! I had abandoned my poor team to an evening of trouble. Our contract calls for hotel accommodation, which can be (and often is) commuted into private hospitality where this is reasonably comfortable. This year the ffolliotts took it upon themselves to vet the bedroom list and dictate that two of the company, who choose to sleep together in the absence of their partners, must be separated. This plan was, of course, doomed to failure, but it caused a lot of ill-will. Love had its way, laughing at locksmiths and ffolliotts alike, as it always will in a house with corridors, but it was perhaps unfortunate that this energetic couple should have met in the room immediately above the ffolliotts' own bedroom.

It is easy to underestimate the problems of life on the road. Often we leave London at lunchtime on Monday, put on six separate performances staying in six different houses, and return to London very late on Saturday night. This formula continues weekly from the end of April, when rehearsals finish, until the beginning of December. Listening to the general chatter, it often seems as if home life can deteriorate into one good row every Sunday. It's easy for me, having been effectively single throughout, but I am very sympathetic to those in the company who try to maintain an orderly home life, and indeed to those who weaken, too. I don't suppose our life is greatly different from that of travelling salesmen or other itinerant entertainers, except that we carry with us an infinity of choice for those feeling isolated; the seeds, if you like, of our own fall. It is actually one of the brighter aspects of the tour, the sense of camaraderie that grows during the season. Just as northern communities tend to be much more supportive than those in the London commuter belts so we, wholly isolated in a long series of alien environments, tend to grow closer, rather than apart. It makes those alien environments, other people's houses, foreign museums, whatever, much more enjoyable, when round every corner I meet familiar faces, hear familiar laughter.

November 27

The last performance of this tour. Kitty is getting married so Bruce Carter, her deputy, will take over next year. Despite our rows, I shall miss her. Reliable, dangerous, vivid, she has been stimulating company.

The Assembly Hall in Stamford has a grand set of restored chandeliers, but it's a bleak room when filled with plastic chairs. I got there far too early and sat smoking in the car, watching people hurrying home in the dark. Finally, I couldn't bear it any more and walked about to visit the great churches – All Saints, golden and crocketed, St Mary's with its massive broach spire, St George's looking rather ill-kempt. Then down the hill and past the George Hotel. Looking in through a lighted window I saw two of the cast, huddled together by a blazing fire. They were both in tears, she in a chair, he kneeling beside her, their faces scarred with misery. I hurried on, embarrassed at having witnessed their sorrow. Tomorrow she must resume her life as another man's wife, he as someone else's husband. Which idiot can ever have said that absence makes the heart grow fonder? The reverse is true. It is support, companionship, sharing love that keeps relationships alive.

November 29

Palm Beach – with Phyllida Fellowes, my overseas organizer, in search of work. The biggest question for any business is how to get work. I just don't believe that people hire something as potentially disastrous as opera from a pretty piece of paper, whether advertisement or brochure. Perhaps my doubts come from having put on concerts at home. The artists I had heard myself were consistent and good, the ones I was persuaded to try by a well-worded agent's letter were uniformly frightful. I would rather feel that my clients know what they are in for before we sign any contracts.

And, indeed, this is how most of our work arises. People in the audience see what we do, think about it, and decide to engage us. That is the ideal – we want to work, they want to employ us – pretty straightforward stuff.

But occasionally my nerve fails. The telephone is silent, huge black holes stare from the diary. The prospect of pouring out regular cheques unsupported by any income (grimly reminiscent of farming) spurs me on to try to promote us.

And then I set off – usually with Phyllida, whose enthusiastic sparkle, natural *bonhomie* and overseas contacts are often crucial – to talk to people who might be interested. If nothing comes of it, she is a marvellous companion for a long journey. Our clients fall into three categories, with one thing in common – a sense of joy in opera. They are confident personalities with access to a beautiful building, or they are responsible for raising money for a charity, or they are in charge of a festival, or the corporate entertaining of a large company.

Opera is a complex form of entertainment, which relies on a suspension of disbelief based on the emotional power of music. It also lasts a long time: at least two hours, sometimes three. That is an *age* to be cooped up, in a room or in a theatre, if the music is poor, the acting embarrassing or the execution amateurish. Some of this can be subjective, with one man laughing at what makes another wince; but there is, I think, an objective standard of taste which an audience is entitled to expect. This is what consumers, ours or anyone else's, need to be reassured of, before committing themselves to a potential personal disaster.

So, here we are. We sent telegrams to our three contacts but no one has returned our telephone calls despite this initial encouragement. Feeling unwanted, we spent the day bicycling round the bay. We had lunch at the Breakers, a hideous Italianate mass, eight storeys high. We bravely bicycled up to the front door and padlocked the bikes to the stone balustrade, before padding up the steps past bemused doormen. Very gloomy.

November 30

Miami – even less response. Our host wasn't home so we were left alone in his palatial wooden bungalow in the middle of a private floodlit swamp. Phyllida found his gymnasium – an underground garage full of well-oiled machines for exercising

various muscles. She loved it. I thought it all rather obscene, a
Piranesian vision of potential torture. The beds had bugs and the
lights were pre-programmed.

December 1

I was woken up by banging somewhere in the house.
I eventually found that Phyllida had managed to lock herself into
the gymnasium. She was remarkably calm, and said the
machines all work perfectly.

December 2

Goodbye to America with no contracts at all. We spent today
looking for the Huntington Hartford Museum, because I wanted
to see Gainsborough's *Blue Boy*. The taxi driver at Los Angeles
airport had never even heard of the museum. But he did have a
map. So between us all, we made it. And the picture is
wonderful – perhaps the best portrait I have ever seen. I really
cannot believe the story that Hartford unwrapped it, stared at it
and then sent an indignant wire to Duveen: 'It's not blue
enough!' The whole picture reeks of blue-ness – dark blue,
bright blue, it dominates the entire gallery with its blue majesty.

December 5

Sydney. Thank God for Jane Austen. I bought them, all six, in a
ramshackle bookshop on the so-called Venice water front (it also
provided me with Colette and Edith Wharton, and Dostoevsky
for Phyllida) just beyond the weight-lifters and the teenage

street-dancers. This flight is a long time to spend in any sort of position.

Things are looking up, here. We drove out three hours to Mesara, a modern Greek revival mansion being completed by our potential employers. It sits on a hilltop in the Australian Cotswolds – the mink and manure belt, so they say. The room will hold one hundred, and they are interested. My friend in Sydney, Di Jagelman, a beautiful dynamo with strawberry-blonde hair, whisked me off to meet Eileen Bond (ditto but with red hair), and she will take the second night if the first couple sign. The lawn here has turned purple – smothered in jacaranda blossom.

December 7

Perth. Staying with Walter Scott, my oldest friend and my eldest son Harry's godfather. The Bonds' house is fine – lots of large Australian landscapes mixed with Old Masters and a huge collection of new cars (three Rolls Royces, et cetera) under one gigantic roof. The Bowral clients sent a message to say that the contract is being flown over after us. When we went swimming in the ocean, the only other person in sight was Jimmy Edwards, rather frail but unmistakably mustachioed. Would he have wanted to be accosted, to be told how much he had made us laugh? We thought not.

December 10th

Kuala Lumpur. 'I had travelled up to visit an old friend, Jane Corsellis, a pretty woman with a shy smile. Her husband, Colonel Corsellis, had gone up country to visit some plantations, so we were alone apart from one other guest – a Mrs

Fellowes, a striking-looking woman with piercing blue eyes, a beautiful complexion and an air of brisk, even challenging determination. She had arrived that morning, carrying all her own baggage, and immediately undertaking to teach the ayah how best to press her linen. Even now, as I sat on the verandah, smoking the last of my black cheroots, and watching the heavy rain turn to steam, I could hear the two women arguing softly on the terrace below.'

Yes, this is authentic Somerset Maugham country. There are great white fans revolving in the rooms, a cobra was found in a flower pot last week, and brightly-swathed Malays pass and repass in front of the compound gates.

Our trip to Singapore has drawn a blank – lovely colonial architecture in amongst very imaginative skyscrapers, but our potential Chinese employer has backed out after making us sit up all night on his bed watching a video of him performing Gilbert and Sullivan. (His wife sat next door, grinning with rage.)

December 11

After three sweltering hours visiting unsuitable buildings, we found the *perfect* one: a Palladian villa, highly ornate, now obviously a brothel but capable (it seems) of being hired for the evening without its smiling inhabitants. I paced out the upper gallery, watched by startled eyes from behind the curtained doorways. It will seat one hundred and thirty-six, plus us, plus a grand piano. There was some giggling.

'What would you like to do now?' asked Jane and Phyllida, as we all walked down the stairs.

December 14

Hong Kong. It's difficult to guess if anything will come of Kuala Lumpur. As usual we have a room but no employer. Once, in Madrid, I had two employers and no room. I stayed for three weeks, going from one building to another trying to find a good environment for *Don Pasquale*. My favourite was a half-restored Baroque church off the Playa Major, but it had no floor, despite its splendidly-restored dome and chipped, scorched pilasters. In the end I settled for the Hotel Velasquez – the apotheosis of oak panelling and red plush.

Hong Kong is quite different. I've spent two days here reading on a sofa because the climate is too much for me. As we were leaving I went to lunch with Emma Keswick, an old friend I hadn't seen for years.

'What on earth are you trying to do?' she asked me.

'Sell an opera performance.'

'How much?'

I told her, and that afternoon she signed a contract for two shows, before dropping me at the airport. So: two in Australia, two in Hong Kong – and Karachi still to go.

December 16

Karachi. Nearly home. We stopped off for one night in Delhi to see some of the buildings. Getting out of the airport at 2 a.m. was an experience – first the endlessly obstructive officials, and then the crowds of bearded porters, snatching at our baggage and jostling each other. When we did get a taxi it was stopped at the perimeter by some soldiers camped round little fires and swathed in heavy brown blankets. They pointed rifles at us.

'What is your name?' asked the driver.

'Stockdale,' I said firmly.

He repeated this and one of the soldiers nodded gravely, and waved us on.

The hotel was my fault. Offered the Oberoi, or a simpler hotel, I had opted for local colour. The water was brown, there was no lock on my door and we had to negotiate what seemed to be a dead body in the corridor. The serenity of the Mughal tombs was almost as soothing as the deliberately deformed child beggars were shocking.

Karachi by contrast is cheerful and bright, with buses decorated in tinfoil, and radios blaring out music. A local heiress is getting married next week, so her family compound round the corner is covered in flags and bunting, with crowds already gathering and bursts of gunfire, presumably in celebration.

John Cowasjee had prudently assembled two sponsors to underwrite his costs. We had lunch with them today and Phyllida photographed them handing over their cheques to me. So we are on – all I need to do now is to deliver the goods.

December 22

How nice to be back.

Pavilion Opera is nothing if not a team. During the performances, I am convinced that our success rests on Bryan's musical genius. In the office, I am equally convinced that it is Christine Baxter's administrative skills that have built us up to our present position. Like me, she dislikes fancy labels, and if asked would probably say that she was my secretary. But this is secretary as in Secretary of State.

She came to Thorpe Tilney in 1977 as Farm Secretary, and watched appalled as the overdraft mounted and as one employee after another had to leave. My policy of choosing labour-intensive crops to keep our staff of seventeen together was a total disaster. After eighteen years, all but three had gone. This paternalistic approach sounded good, but we all lost out in the end. If I am accused now of too rough and ready a way with employees, I can at least point to a paradox: the increasing number of jobs that I am able to offer.

Who can guess at Christine's feelings as the Pavilion was planned and built, a fairly complicated and expensive mixture of brickwork, carving, plasterwork, wrought iron and stained glass, roofed with weathered tiles removed from the cows' winter shed?

Nevertheless, she persevered, and since the painful process of paying off the banks and the Inland Revenue has been gradually completed thanks to the Opera's success, it is she who has constantly warned me against repeating my mistakes in farming. She is, in fact, my main bulwark against the demands of others.

'Oh, Freddie?' The producer or the designer is speaking.

'Yes?'

'We just need an extra session tomorrow night on *Così*.' Or an extra costume. Or six new wigs. Or our own van.

An impresario's life sometimes seems to consist of nothing more creative than saying No! And I can say it because I know Christine would disapprove if I said Yes.

That's one side. The other is even more important. While we lounge about in the Home Counties, or sit waiting in a French hotel, it is Christine who is by the telephone, talking to our clients, encouraging, explaining, organizing and reassuring them to keep our progress smooth. Most of the British contracts are made by her. Her cool brand of incisive but sympathetic efficiency literally keeps the show on the road.

Today she has come to London to spend two days: the farm is still operating in a partnership, I am approaching the deadline of a book of Opera synopses, and the inevitable problems of our old buildings need solutions. There is much to do.

December 23

Chaos – Christine and I catching up with overdue post, Christmas shopping and trying to complete the book on opera. We're living in a dense fog of cigar smoke, fumbling our way through the 'S'es. Strauss has been fun – but Stravinsky! How I hate *The Rake's Progress*. I'd forgotten what a killer it is. In fact, when I put it on the gramophone to rekindle my worst memories, it sounded more bestial than usual.

Christine stared at the speakers. 'Are you sure you've got the right speed?'

There was nothing on the label. I was playing it at 33.

'Let's try 45 r.p.m.'

It sounded worse.

My machine can even cope with 78, but that sounded beyond belief. No – now we shall never know. But my synopsis for the book is coolly subjective, I think.

January 8

I spent most of Christmas working on the *Figaro* and *Don Giovanni* scores. They are nearly complete. New Year is the moment for my children to congregate at Thorpe Tilney with as many friends as can be crammed in.

Thorpe Tilney is, to me, a very pretty house, early Georgian, in a lovely faded red brick. Flanked by stables and other ancillary buildings, it is a wooded oasis within the fen. Either you like flat countryside, or you don't. Luckily I do; I find the empty wastes, dominated by a vast sky and unexpectedly filled with wild life, intensely romantic. Of course, they cannot compete with the Bavarian Alps or the Scottish Borders, but in their own way, they have great beauty.

My wife and I bought the house and farm when we were engaged. She subsequently became more attached to another house we had acquired, and now lives there. There was no garden at Thorpe Tilney when we arrived, and the park trees had been deliberately and systematically destroyed. Everything had been ploughed up.

With the current decline in agriculture I have started trying to put things back, even to improve on the original. After twenty years, the garden is now beginning to take a settled shape. Some people suffer from a painful disease called Spreading Flowerbeds: I suffer from a much less obtrusive one called Elongating Avenues. The main one has now got down to the river, which is pretty pointless as it is completely out of sight. HOWEVER, if I can get the costs past Christine, I am now plotting inter-connecting *allées* and a *rond-point*. And more clumps. I can't remember if some sage said that man is seldom so innocently employed as when chasing women or money. I would have thought gardening, even from a distance as I have to do it, is an even more harmless occupation.

But now the school holidays are over, and it is back to work.

January 10

Lunch with Jon Pither, Chairman of Amari. We first met him at Pyrford Court near Woking with Cyril and Valerie Laikin, our most frequent employers. He just came up after a performance to say how much he had enjoyed it.

'Do you have trouble balancing the books?' he asked.

Those were the days when a balance was the best I could hope for.

'Here's my number,' he said, handing me a card. 'Ring Jennie and we'll talk about it.'

Five years later, I still don't really know what he does. But I do know he runs a happy office, full of contented cheerful people whose natural reaction to a stranger is a welcoming smile.

Today it's just four of us, Jon, Jennie his assistant, Phyllida and me, swapping stories about last year. They're going to sponsor *Don Giovanni* this year, which means their name will be attached to each performance and credited on the tickets and so on.

'What did we give you last year?' he asked.

I told him.

'Well, let's make it X,' he said, adding another £5000.

This means I can now safely employ the two musicians dressed as Don Giovanni's servants, to play in the party scenes.

January 11

The main problem over Roberto is that he comes from the Commonwealth. After all, I managed to get a work permit for Blair from America. I even got one for Sobhi Bidair from Egypt. But the *Commonwealth*? Oh, no, I'm afraid not.

But friends are trying. Principally David Heathcoat Amory, who is an MP in the west country and marvellously patient when I telephone him daily about this.

We had some more auditions today. Three camp Don Giovannis, one with a bulging belly, two who looked like Rigolettos and one who couldn't get the high notes. How do you explain this to permanent officials? On the other hand, we heard an excellent Lucia, whom we don't need.

January 13

A day looking at houses. First Blenheim with James Garson for the Boys' Clubs, then Heythrop, and the Faringdons' other house at Barnsley, and back to London via Clandon outside Guildford.

Blenheim, where we are planning one of our orchestral performances, is superb – a true palace. No wonder the Churchills are a proud family. The view from the front door, great heaps of beautiful golden stone in every direction carved, ornamented, regimented and shining in the sunlight. How could one expect them to relate to their contemporaries?

The Comptroller (often a bad sign) was full of little tips.

'The orchestra must be in place ten minutes before the performance.'

'Why?' I asked.

'So they can stand up when their Graces enter.'

Now, no one stands up in this way except for royalty, but he was absolutely adamant.

'The Duke insists on this,' he said angrily.

Can this really be true? I wonder.

In the end I was reduced to the lowest common denominator – money.

'Oh, well, we'll do it if you insist. But it will cost an extra – oh – eight hundred pounds, I would guess.' More anger.

'That's not in the contract!'

'Paragraph seven. Overtime. Ten minutes for an orchestra is quite a chunk. Anyway, let me know.' Goodness knows if the musicians will agree, but my guess is that the plan will be dropped.

Heythrop is an ill-fated house, burnt twice and now in the hands of the NatWest after the usual desecration by the Jesuits, only surpassed by the notorious Claretian Fathers under whose auspices Highcliffe Castle was burnt to the ground. Despite the unforgivable additions and plate-glass windows, the house is obviously well cared for. An odd mistake is the central bay on the north front, where the broken pediment has recently been restored back to front, giving it an absurdly comical air.

Barnsley is a sleeping beauty, hidden in the woods above the village and used in the summer. It is late Baroque, possibly by

Smith of Warwick, with a magnificent stuccoed Hall which will hold one hundred and twenty at a pinch. It is like a slightly reduced model of Clandon, whose giant Hall will hold two hundred if they're crammed in, one hundred and fifty in comfort. A minor problem at Clandon about where we should change, but with an excellently helpful administrator, I am reasonably hopeful we shall end up in the Library. Anyone can understand the National Trust's cautious attitude towards the houses they maintain. It is right, but sensible compromises can be reached.

January 14

Up betimes, since I have to look at Yorkshire houses. Castle Howard is difficult. The Vanbrugh Hall, with its colossal orders, is as unsuitable as the Blenheim Hall is perfect. Surprisingly, it is also too small. The Robinson wing has a large plain Palladian room of stupendous dreariness. There probably are good rooms in the burnt bit, but they were off-limits. I met the new administrator at Beningbrough where we return twice this year, saw the splendid Drawing-room at Aske (a hundred and fifty to a hundred and sixty if we use raised seating), and finally paid my annual pilgrimage to Sutton Scarsdale, the beautiful ruin on a hilltop to the west of the M1. Without their balusters the balustrades now look like battlements, and the jungle is taking over. It is the Cold Lairs of the Midlands, and none the worse for that.

January 15

Sir Rupert de la Bère was Lord Mayor of London at the Coronation. He muffed his lines at the rehearsal and earned a stinging rebuke from his deceptively mild-looking sovereign.

The man who used to call him every morning told me that each day's conversation was the same: Sir Rupert would ask him, as he drew back the curtains,

'Tell me, Frederick, who is the most brilliant, best-looking and funniest man you know?'

'You, Sir Rupert.' A nod of satisfaction from the bed, and the Lord Mayor was ready to face his day.

Whenever I look particularly down in the dumps, Bryan says kindly: 'I don't know how you manage.' (At least, I *think* he means it kindly . . .)

How can I put into words the sheer fun and joyousness of our rural tours? Of course we have rows, of course we mooch about with grumbling faces, but the overall picture is one of terrific excitement, a busy scene framed within the beauty of the countryside and the great houses which rear up behind crumbling perimeter walls in every county.

I had, for example, never visited Shropshire before we took the opera to Attingham. Housman's poetry, gladly learnt at school, took on new loveliness as some of us walked among the falling leaves on Wenlock Edge. And curiously enough, the spirit of the Romans seems very real in the remoter parts of England, and not only when, as on 'Capability' Brown's great terrace at Sledmere, a massive centurion stares stonily out across the valley towards the softly ordered contours of the beeches on the farther bank.

If much of our time is spent relentlessly clocking up monotonous miles on the motorways, the best times take us through the little winding lanes that connect those dreary thoroughfares to the hidden villages in the hills. Only sixty years ago, these lanes would still have been unmetalled – simple earthen tracks, used only to the slow progress of cattle and an occasional horse-drawn cart. A single generation has seen that peace swept away by the fierce invasion of the motor car. At first it must have seemed a great adventure – the freedom to travel farther and farther within a single day. Now, our capacity to cover hundreds of miles a day in search of someone willing to pay us for entertainment has come at the price of emptying those lanes of all but the bravest pedestrians. Children are no longer safe, as I was, to bicycle loosely round those blind corners, overgrown with brambles, the whole road shrouded in green as the trees were left free to join together in vaults of natural growth.

I have always been in love with the English country house. The châteaux of France seem too overbearing, the palaces of Italy far too garish, and it is very difficult to think of German castles as homes. But in England, from the romance in miniature of Great Chalfield to the Baroque spendour of Easton Neston, there is a modesty and a feeling of art used for family enjoyment which is particularly appealing. As a matter of fact, the inquisitive follower of Pavilion Opera can get a very thorough picture of English architecture through a season, starting with the fortified castles of the Norman period, such as Rockingham and Powderham, and moving on, through medieval manor houses like Hill Deverill until, with the end of the Wars of the Roses, it was safe again to build in timber (Rufford Old Hall, 1540) and brick (Layer Marney).

The Tudors brought great prosperity, opening up the world's trade by control of the sea, and this is reflected in the giant palaces like Hatfield. Most building stopped during the Civil War, thus robbing us of what Inigo Jones might have created, but with the Restoration came new confidence. At Petworth, the Proud Duke of Somerset created a house at the crossroads of the old and the new – harking back to the medieval dominance of house over town, while looking forward to the next century in its great rolling park, later to be further improved by 'Capability' Brown. At the same time its contemporary, Ragley, was already being built in a domain of its own, and by the end of the century the new fashion for great houses, remote in their solitary rural grandeur, was well established.

Continental ideas were gradually becoming accepted: French (Petworth), Dutch (Blickling) and Italian (Burley-on-the-Hill), all assimilated into the gloriously rich cocktail of an evolving

78

style of grand domestic architecture that scattered the whole of England with large, comfortable buildings which until the end of the eighteenth century provided related employment for more than seventy per cent of the entire population. Theirs was the golden age of Baroque and Palladian architecture: Beningbrough, Attingham, Kedleston, Gorhambury, Wardour, Sledmere, Basildon.

A moment's pause to deal with Napoleon, and building started again with renewed enthusiasm in the early years of the nineteenth century. At Wynyard, when Lord Londonderry's new and immense house was gutted by fire while he was abroad on his honeymoon, a nervous message to this effect received the reply 'Rebuild forthwith'.

Throughout the nineteenth century, financed by 'new' money, cheap coal and great confidence, huge new houses (Thoresby, Capesthorne) rocketed up to amaze their neighbours.

Since all these styles involved large rooms for entertaining, we can find ourselves a niche somewhere in any such building. Long galleries (Blickling, Osterley) are the most difficult: our style of performance only works if we can act in and make use of the architecture of the room without any form of staging, which immediately creates a destructively theatrical feel.

Halls (Beningbrough, Clandon, Gorhambury, Burley) are ideal as being square, and staircases (Cricket, Leigh Court, Sledmere) can be spectacular if suited to the opera; but drawing-rooms (Aske, Petworth, Moor Place), picture galleries (Attingham) and dining-rooms (Kedleston) are equally good, and we now often seem to find ourselves in barns, cathedrals, City Halls and hotels.

January 16

Another day in the office struggling with the accounts. They're pretty simple. Ninety per cent of our income comes from opera fees (of which one third is overseas earnings), so much per performance, the balance from just three sources: programme sales, the Friends' subscriptions, and commercial sponsorship by three companies. They pay me some money, I seek to promote their business by giving them publicity and the opportunity for personalized corporate entertainment. It's a happy relationship – Sotheby's and Amari have just signed on for their fifth year, Octavian Underwriting for their seventh.

On the spending side, about seventy per cent goes on wages, fifteen per cent on travelling (mainly overseas) and fifteen per cent on the overheads – costumes, props, the office and rehearsal rooms. On income, we aim for a margin of fifteen per cent; sometimes we get it, sometimes we don't. It's very easy to be undercut when all your competitors (at home and overseas) demand and get large chunks of public money. But that's also what gives us our impetus. We know we *have* to earn our wages. There is no comforting Nanny to run to if our work isn't good enough to pay its way. Either we're good enough, or we go out of business. And I believe this is a powerful motivation to spur us to success, just as the opposite drags some other companies down.

Do you remember Rocco (Edward G. Robinson) in Huston's film *Key Largo*? Asked by the exasperated heroine (Lauren Bacall) what he really wants, he looks flummoxed. The hero (Humphrey Bogart) steps in: 'How about "more"? Perhaps you want more.'

Rocco's face clears.

'Yeah! That's it!' he grins. 'More, I want more.'

There are quite a few Roccos in the opera world.

To be fair, the older ones, Sir Rocco This and Lord Rocco of That, have spent their whole lives assuming that opera is a public service rather than a business. Like old British Leyland, perhaps, or the erstwhile British Steel Corporation. After all, it wasn't so long ago we were all told that mining for coal (a major nineteenth-century source of fortunes) had become a protected hobby, like morris dancing.

January 17

A quick trip back to Holland to perform *Don Pasquale* at the
Mauritshuis. It's a beautiful square house built right on the water
by the old Palace. Along with the Frick and the Wallace
Collection, it is one of the most welcoming of museums. Not
too big, but with a superb collection: three great Vermeers,
including his *View of Delft* whose patch of yellow so fascinated
Bergotte. In our changing room are four Holbeins, which were
among the disputed pictures removed from England by William
III. He did quite a bit of moving paintings around in the general
refurnishing of Hampton Court, Kensington Palace and Het
Loo. When he died, the British Crown tried to get about twenty
back from Holland. We were just about to have a major row
(with some sabre-rattling) when the War of the Austrian
Succession surfaced to make it suddenly impolitic to press the
point. But those paintings haven't been forgotten, and now form
part of that fascinating group of historical grumbles which
includes Gibraltar, the Elgin Marbles, and now the private
palaces of Eastern Europe.

January 18

The Hague. Absolute panic. Enid lost her voice this morning.
   Occasionally the singers make a joke out of it.
   'Hello, Noel, how are you?'
   '   '. He opens his mouth and no sound emerges.
   'Eh?' I try to pretend my heart hasn't stopped.
   A terrible groaning whisper: 'I'm all right . . . I think.' Then
he roars with laughter. I always fall for it, every time.
   But today it's true. And it's too late to fly her understudy
over. Luckily it's a tiny part (the Notary). I make an
announcement and the audience look slightly restive. But truly I
don't think it mattered. She croaked away, but acted excellently.

And the others were wonderful – Susan and Blair putting in extra verve to shift the focus.

Afterwards the Mauritshuis Foundation gave us all dinner, and announced an encouraging profit for the Museum. The bigger, the better for us; it makes them more likely to employ us again next year. I walked back through the empty streets, to where I am staying with Maxine and Michael Jenkins.

What I like about Bruce Rankin's performances is the concentrated imagination and sincerity which he brings to them, coupled with his natural wit which bubbles up irrepressibly in the comedies. He has a wide range, from his jealous, castrated Ottavio, his sadistic, Neronic Duke, to tonight's simple-minded Ernesto, or the manic exuberance of his Eisenstein, crying with laughter as he retells the story of his practical joke, oblivious of the enigmatic reaction of his avenging victim. He is always totally believable, totally absorbing.

January 19

David Heathcoat Amory rang to say the relevant Minister has rejected Roberto's application.

'Oh, God!' I said. This really was a disaster.

'No! No!' he said. 'It isn't over yet. Just leave it with me.'

He is wonderfully persistent. But what will I do without a convincing Don? He is the pivot of the whole opera – the driving force. However well the others sing, a clammy, pouting Don Giovanni can't help but wreck the plot. As I have often witnessed. Compare such a travesty with Rugiero Raimondi, or William Shimell, or any other great exponent of the role. At least I have an excellent understudy in Arthur Coomber, but he is also singing Rigoletto. He can't do everything!

Why are all attractive women already married? I sat next to someone called Anne Barclay last night. We chatted away about

Mrs Gaskell, whom I've never read, and then Turgenev. She'd just read *The Torrents of Spring*, so that kept us going. I was explaining Turgenev's theory about crystallization – namely, that love performs on the desired one the same effect that the Siberian winter has on a branch left down a salt mine. Suddenly it is covered with a myriad tiny twinkling lustres, white and wholly beautiful to the admiring eye. Expanding on this, I suddenly realized I had been gazing too long into her hazel eyes, at her full dark lips. In short, I was sitting next to a fully encrusted Siberian branch.

'This is Tony,' she said, introducing me to her husband, a young man with a rather clockwork manner. He shook my hand briskly. I could see we weren't destined to be soul mates.

'How nice to meet you,' I said cosily.

He gave a sort of snort.

Tony Barclay

January 20

Today I went to look at North Mymms Park, the intriguing
Jacobean house that lurks in the woodlands west of the A1 near
Hatfield. It had a famous rose garden laid out by an American
heiress. I knew it had been bought from her son by developers.
Now it has been taken over by Elders, the Australian company
headed by John Elliott in whose Melbourne apartment I had
stayed, even though I've never met him.

You can see the mis-matched lodges from the motorway, but
they're difficult to reach through the maze of side roads.

'Mr Stockdale?'

It was my potential employer, a short forthright man in his
mid fifties, no doubt the Chairman of the charity. We went in to
meet the caretaker, a tall gaunt man with a rather hunted
expression.

'You're John's chum?'

'Yes, indeed,' I said, hoping he wouldn't ask when I'd last
seen him.

'What about this, then?' He showed me into a long low room.
It had a pair of hideous tarantula chandeliers, a rather smelly
nylon carpet – nothing else. I clapped my hands. Dead!

'Urrgh,' I said.

'Do you want the job or don't you?' snapped the Chairman.

It was my fault, I suppose, for being too blunt, and also on
too short a fuse to cope with others' bluntness. However, I was
able to concentrate on the caretaker.

'Surely there's a wonderful set of tapestries? Where are they?'

And of course we found a splendid room upstairs, with a tall
ceiling and nice resonant acoustics despite the famous tapestries.

'This will seat a hundred and fifty,' I said after pacing it out.

'We're having two hundred,' said the Chairman to the
caretaker.

Sometimes I think it would be easier to turn this sort of job
down, but we need the business.

'May I explain?' I said, trying to keep calm. 'You can get a hundred and fifty by having three rows on the long side, four rows at either end, and two blocks of ten on either side of the piano. If you have any more, the people at the back simply won't see. Your guests would rather pay £50 each for a hundred and fifty tickets than £35 each for two hundred tickets, and you'll still make the same amount of money.'

Silence.

'Unless, of course,' I added unwisely, 'you raise the seats on pallets at the back.'

'We've got a stage,' said the caretaker, 'somewhere in the building.'

'That's it,' said the Chairman, still not looking at me. 'The opera can be raised on the stage.'

'I'm afraid that's not possible,' I said.

'Why not?'

'Because we never do. It loses its point and looks like a boxing bout.'

'I'll talk to his Head Office,' he said, turning away to the caretaker, who winked at me.

I can see this is going to be tricky.

January 22

Touring opera is like playing bridge. Each performance is different, even though the fomula and ingredients remain the same.

If we perform, as we usually do, at six different houses in the week, sometimes we will do six nights of the same opera (switching casts intermittently), or sometimes six diffeerent operas. It all depends on the employers.

The day starts with a late breakfast. The first to leave is the blue seven-ton wardrobe lorry with Colin at the wheel. He will have been finishing off the washing in the morning (all the shirts

BEFORE THE SHOW

and tights, every day) and has to get to the new house in time to press all the costumes for the evening. This year he has an assistant, Nicky Jackson, very patient and methodical. He has the costumes of six shows on board in case of disasters, plus a spare set of lights.

Next to go will be the stage management lorry, with Bruce Carter at the wheel. He has Nicky Whitsun-Jones (last year's Assistant Stage Manager) beside him as his deputy, and Matt Muller as his assistant. They have the carpet, six sets of props, the main lights and a formidable array of equipment for repairing, rewiring or replacing anything that goes wrong. Plus the all-important tea basket, for which they will buy fresh milk and biscuits *en route*. They also need to get there early – to check the layout and accommodation, unroll the carpet and set up the lights. Colin will already have taken possession of the changing room – sometimes our host's bedroom, sometimes an Adam dining-room – in order to lay out the steamed and ironed costumes, and freshly laundered shirts.

It is this vanguard that sets the tone of our invasion. Colin and Bruce are both masters of diplomacy. No one could take exception to the quiet tact with which they monopolize our employers' living spaces. It hasn't always been like this! In the early days I used to have to get there first in order to mediate. Now I can drift along quietly, reaching the house about four o'clock. We all have mobile telephones so they can alert me or Bryan if there is a problem.

'Freddie?'

'Yes?'

'Bruce here. I'm afraid they've blocked the second exit with chairs and say they can't be moved.'

This is quite usual.

'Is our employer there?' I ask.

'No – he's out shooting, but the housekeeper is most insistent.'

'Don't worry. Leave it till he gets back.'

'Right-oh.'

And when I arrive, it's already been shifted and everyone is smiling. After all, we all want to make a success of the performance. Sometimes priorities get misplaced – especially by caterers; at Adlington, for example, the Legh's medieval house in Cheshire built round their original tree, we came back from tea to find the room full of stinking steam – they had moved all the costumes and started cooking vegetables on a hitherto unremarked stove. Most, however, are amenable to reason.

Because of a horror of communal changing, I tend now to wear a black suit. It looks a bit odd on country mornings, but it has the great advantage of being able to double as dark suit or dinner jacket, simply by changing the tie. Phyllida doesn't approve, but I really don't think anyone else notices.

Then, at about 4.30, the singers begin to arrive. Some, like Noel, are always early, some scrupulously punctual, and some of course are always late. Lateness matters for two reasons: our half-hour rehearsal is essential to sort out the doors and distances, and it is grossly discourteous to their colleagues who have made the effort to be on time. This period also anchors, by running through the dialogue, which opera we are doing, and gives Bryan a chance to tighten up any musical sloppiness. This is the moment of truth – are they all here, are they all fit and well?

Then comes dinner, that crucial ingredient of our joint contracts – theirs with me, mine with our employers. It needs to be hot and ample, whatever the weather. For most of the crew it is the main meal of the day, sometimes the only one, if they've spent a well-earned morning in bed. It gives them the energy they need for the performance, at a time when I am usually too nervous to eat (unless there's ice-cream or treacle pudding).

Then comes an hour or more of getting ready. The stage crew are getting out the programmes and checking the props for the third and last time, the singers are putting on costumes, wigs and make-up, and I am pacing up and down, with a soothing cigar if I'm lucky, with a face of torture if not. Our employer is probably having a bath and getting changed, bottles are being opened, the piano tuner may have come back for a final check. Somewhere in a back corridor a singer is warming up with a few vocal exercises. The house is alive with tension and activity.

The front door opens. Guests start arriving all at once, and we're on the inexorable count-down.

'This is your half-hour call,' announces Bruce, thirty-five minutes before the appointed hour. Regularly he chants the dwindling minutes. Then the audience begin to move in and take their seats.

'Beginners!' Bryan takes his place outside the door. Bruce and I check the gangways and I sit down by the piano. Two latecomers hurry in, one of them looking flustered and the other cross. The lights dim. We're off.

Afterwards the singers throw off their soaking clothes – Colin and Nicky will wash some of them that night in our portable machine. I talk to people in the audience – there's usually someone who wants to know what it costs, what dates we have free. My host brings me a drink and sometimes sends some wine in for the cast. Two of the stage crew will be unobtrusively dismantling the lights while the third stands guard on the dressing room door. There's often an over-zealous member of the audience who wants to talk to the girl or man of his or her dreams, forgetting that the others are stark naked and want some privacy. Occasionally I have to be called to eject them.

Years ago our then Barber of Seville suffered from a woman who, having seen him at a performance, followed us all round the country, spending hundreds of pounds on tickets. He consistently refused even to talk to her, so every night I had to try to explain to her that however flattered we all were, this particular man needed to stay very quiet after a show. In the end, I begged him at least to go for a walk with her. Sadly, she didn't come again after that.

By eleven o'clock we're ready to go – back home if we're in London, slowly up to bed if we're deep in the countryside. The singers will have drifted off as soon as they finished. Last of all will be the two lorries. Theirs is a long hard day – every day. But they're still cheerful and considerate – after all, we all want to come back next year.

If we're in a hotel, there will be a party in somebody's bedroom. Everyone contributes – wine, beer, crisps, sandwiches even. It's always fun, and wherever we are most of us need a couple of hours to unwind, for the adrenalin to settle down after the charge of the performance. But by one o'clock everyone will be tucked up, singly or together – because tomorrow will be the same, and the day after, for months to come.

AFTER THE SHOW

January 23

Two weeks' holiday in Barbados. A welcome prospect –
finishing off the synopses, mulling over the new productions,
but principally relaxing. And I've even got the excuse that Bryan
is cruising in the Caribbean and his ship will be calling at
Barbados on the 30th. So we plan to meet for lunch and
compare notes.

January 30

Pavilion Opera's Caribbean board meeting was good fun. Bryan
appeared at the hotel pool and he and I went off to lunch in his
gigantic ship, before walking round the quay discussing
Roberto's chances. He looks sunburnt and happy.

February 5

Absolute panic about Roberto so I flew back yesterday, to find
David's message that the relevant official would see me today. I
got there an hour early this morning and read the papers again
before being shown up to meet the man who would decide
whether our *Don Giovanni* would be a success or a failure. And
he turned out to be charming, a member of an amateur operatic
society and a friend of my previous Equity representative.
What's more, he had Roberto's work permit on his desk. I could
have had two more days on the beach, but I was even happier to
have this permit.

February 10

We all met at Heathrow: Noel, Blair, George, Helen and Alice
to sing, Bryan to play, Bruce Carter to stage manage, Colin
Window to do the wardrobe, Phyllida and me. Colin came to us
in 1984 as the designer's assistant for *Traviata*. He sat cooped up
in the pantry sewing on sequins. When I had to dismiss the stage
manager at short notice, the only person available to take over
was Colin.

'Would you be prepared to take over as stage manager?'

He looked amazed.

'But I've never done anything like that before.'

'Nor have I,' I pointed out. 'But it's got to be one of us two,
and I think you could do it better.'

He evidently saw the force of this argument and agreed. After
three years as stage manager, he asked to be allowed to revert to
wardrobe. He's been in charge of that ever since. Well over six
foot six, very blond and very thin, he is always stared at in
foreign countries where the average height is small. He is also
very mild, and given to self-doubt. But his skill at designing and
making costumes is so evidently outstanding that I find it easy to
reassure him when he occasionally loses heart.

Sydney, Perth, Hong Kong, Karachi – far beyond the reach of
understudies and only one of our employers has ever seen us
perform. We have exactly three weeks to get back in time for
rehearsals – the designer is already running up costumes, the
répétiteurs are coaching the other singers, Christine is drumming
up last-minute contracts to fill the gaps. And best of all – no one
is late for the flight.

February 12

We reached Sydney to find (a) a message from our Sydney
employer to say that he would not be paying for any of our
meals and (b) that the bus he should have ordered was not there!

So after nearly 24 hours of travel we sat down and stared at each other while Phyllida rushed off to do some telephoning.

The Australian customs were quite straightforward. Colin and I went through with the opera cases.

'What's in the box, mate?'

'Long dresses, I *think*.' He gave me a long look, then Colin.

'Are there many of you?'

'Yes – we're here to do an opera.'

He waved us through.

Phyllida finally organized a bus (we have a three-hour drive to get down to Bowral, where we are to spend some time recovering from the flight), and reassured me about the meals.

'It's so clear in the contract. Once I speak to his office, I'm sure it will be okay.'

Well, it wasn't okay in the bus. It duly arrived, but the driver was either drunk or so tired that he couldn't keep awake. There was a sudden scream from Helen, and I looked up to see the nose of the bus veering off the road towards a tree. We all shrieked out, and the driver yanked the wheel round just as we hit the kerb. Noel and I went to sit near him. He dropped off again. Noel hit him on the knee. He hardly reacted, so we made him pull up at a garage.

'One of us will drive,' I said.

'No way.' He was bleary but adamant.

So on we went, Noel prodding him and shouting in his ears whenever necessary. We were really pleased to see the motel sign – meals or no meals. Noel has given up sugar for lent, so we amused ourselves by planning a maple syrup supper after Easter.

February 13

Well, it *was* okay about the meals.

'Just a misunderstanding,' said Phyllida. She'd left us to stay with the Jagelmans (lucky thing). We've been here four days now, and are nearly out of our minds with boredom. Twice a day we troop into Bowral to eat steaks and omelettes. Blair sits by the pool, Alice stays indoors reading, I walk round and round the little paths, working on *Figaro* in my head.

'Would you like a book, Fred–dee?' asks Alice.

'Oh, yes *please*, Alice. What have you got?'

'Just Anita Brookner.'

'Wonderful. How many?'

'Just *A Misalliance*.'

'I'd love to read it again. Thank you very much.'

February 14

Thank God. The performance at last. We have rested for four days, but it wasn't enough. I could sense the strain in the voices, but only because I knew them all so well. Blair was wonderfully funny, and Helen slew the men. The audience were so nice – lots of laughs and lots of encouragement. Di Jagelman brought her butler from Sydney to pass round caviare sandwiches to her party in the interval. And buckets of champagne. Phyllida brought *The Brothers Karamazov* to keep me occupied.

February 20

We had two days in Sydney. One bit of luck was meeting at the performance the man who is hanging the exhibition of pictures from the Hermitage – some of which were the paintings that Sir Robert Walpole's grandson sold from Houghton to Catherine the Great. He asked us to go and have a sneak preview: highlight being a sexy Joshua Reynolds (Cupid untying the very scanty bodice of a Venus who is hiding her face). Also a very pretty Renoir that Phyllida said made her feel sick. The only other person there was Joan Sutherland. I longed to ask her how she coped with jet-travel dehydration. But I felt it would have been an intrusion, so confined myself to platitudes about a vivid Picasso.

February 22

The Bond evening went well. Only a hundred guests, paying A$1000 each. Robert Holmes à Court told Walter he would cheerfully pay A$1000 *not* to come. Anyway, they made a good profit. Eileen Bond was a treat to work for. Everything I asked for was brought instantly, and when she caught one of the cast trying on her Emanuel dress, she merely said, 'Well – it looks better on you than it does on me!' She's also given me a huge hat with flowers and cherries on it because she heard me telling Colin to copy it for our next *Elisir d'amore*.

Now we've reached Hong Kong; our hostesses were aghast to see us traipsing in on the Perth–Bangkok flight looking rather bedraggled.

February 23

Tonight our employers took us off to a local restaurant where they gave us lots of cocktails. The first dish was made up of chicken, with a stuffed cockerel complete with head. George seized this, bit off the head and crunched it up.
    Everyone stared.
    'Was it nice?' I asked him nervously.
    'No,' he whispered, 'but it's what they expect.'
    Not judging by their expressions.

February 24

I think it's in *Persuasion* that the heroine waits eagerly for a letter. But when it arrives, it is far from what she had hoped for. 'I will never hope for news again', she says, or something similar.

It is the same with me. I had been hoping for letters ever since we left. Nothing! But today a telephone call – what utter fools we make of ourselves in projecting our hopes onto others. But no one with children need ever despair.

February 25

Emma and Simon Keswick, with whom I'm staying, have an intriguing view across the water. From here (on the terrace) I have a two-hundred-and-fifty-degree panorama of fifteen gigantic volcanic mountains rearing out of a grey-black sea. There are clouds everywhere, floating on the water, drifting past me, and all lit by a piercing white light.

Immediately below me, hundreds of shadowy white skyscrapers are intermittently revealed through the mist, and the whole scene is accompanied by the eerie hoots of the foghorns of passing ships. It needs Turner to do it justice, or Martin, whose picture *The Last Bard* hangs in the room we perform in Newcastle's Laing Gallery.

Their guard is called 'Mr Goodnight', because whenever you see him, whatever you say, he always replies with solemn courtesy, 'Goodnight'.

February 26

Yesterday we performed at the Hong Kong Academy of Performing Arts to some two hundred students. A nice cheerful audience in a room plain beyond one's wildest nightmares. Later we auditioned some of them – the girls much better than the rather leaden men. Apparently Hong Kong Chinese is different from the mainland language, so they often communicate among themselves in operatic Italian!

Tonight we're in the new house of the Chairman of the Hong Kong Bank. It's perched right on the top of the Peak, swathed in mist but very comfortable.

Emma is looking superb in a stiff-pleated, flared black organza three-quarter-length skirt with a waisted cerise silk jacket. She has raised nearly £100,000 this evening, mostly in donations, for the planned Hospice. Another of her colleagues has just come up:

'I hope your singers are house-trained,' she boomed.

'What?'

'I mean,' she went on,' they *do* know how to tip, I suppose?'

There's caviare everywhere, but the toast has run out. I found a tablespoon and set to.

'I always distrust a man who isn't greedy,' murmured Emma as she led a *Last Emperor* look-alike towards the bar.

So – the performance went smoothly. There were some splendidly inscrutable Chinese billionaires in the front row who were wholly won over by Noel. (Helen they watched out of the corners of their eyes with a sort of horrified, anxious fascination, as if she were a snake trying to hypnotize them.)

February 27

Karachi: it was only on the flight that Phyllida told me she and Alice had had to share a double bed in Hong Kong. What saints they both are. No complaints when there's no solution.

Pakistan customs were not so obliging. Arriving at 2 a.m. in the morning earns you the undivided attention of the night shift. We were met by a British Consulate official, but even so, each customs officer insisted on consulting his superior, so that eventually we reached an enormous pockmarked character with FIVE gold bars on each epaulette and a distinct resemblance to General Woundwort. He brought his entire staff to look at us. Through the plate-glass barrier I could see poor John Cowasgee wilting in the heat and gloom outside, gesticulating at me in dumb mime.

'We will look inside a suitcase,' announced the General.

'Try mine,' suggested Blair brightly.

Well, all I can say is that it looked like a Harrods catalogue. It was simply stuffed with hi-fi sets, Walkmen, boxed sets of silk ties. They couldn't believe their eyes – nor could I! Why on earth had he volunteered?

Of course, after that, every suitcase, every bag had to be opened up and searched. Out came silk costumes, silver inkstands, two old flintlock pistols – everything seemed suddenly suspect. What was worst for me was that I had three laser pistols in my plastic bag which I had bought in Hong Kong for my sons. I had already expostulated about having nothing of value – against Phyllida's insistent advice – but they suddenly lost interest and waved us through to our exhausted hosts.

February 28

The garden of the British Consulate here, which is where the performance is now going to take place, is full of gaunt men in turbans carrying dusty blue burdens which they dump in apparent confusion. There is a vulture sitting in the tree opposite. What is so nice is that these are all really friendly people behind the scowls. Whenever I smile, or raise my hand in greeting, all beam broadly in return, villainous teeth appearing in the curiously lopsided grins. Only the 'vulture' (presumably a kite) has been watching me with unblinking concentration. I have an uneasy feeling that it thinks me agreeably meaty.

All yesterday they were erecting the tent. It is massive, made up of giant panels of scarlet and black and blue and orange zigzags stitched together with thick twine. Last night it arose, like a flapping whale, 20 feet high, 50 feet wide, 100 feet long. I went in alone after dinner and clapped three times. After a pause, there came the echo 'clap – clap!' *Two* claps? It was a nasty moment when I realized that it hadn't been an echo. There was something else in that cavernous darkness. It was – aaargh! No – in fact, it was the nightwatchman, who considerately came and stood immediately behind me, turning on his lamp to reveal bloodshot eyes and a deeply scarred cheek.

'Er – hello,' I said.

His mouth split to give me an excellent view of his tooth (a solitary straggler).

This evening we went to a superb party given by John. I had a breakneck journey there driven by his Christian chauffeur Robin, who careered between the vast buses covered with silver foil and frantic passengers clinging to the running boards on one side, and the tiny rickshaw taxis (like sedan chairs built round mopeds) on the other.

John had covered his garden and drive with bright oriental carpets, and made me take my shoes off. It all looked very lush. When we got to the far end of the garden I saw something over his shoulder: a lorry carrying chairs was starting to reverse very slowly over the carpets.

John turned, shrieked and ran gesticulating towards the four tiny, bearded villains squeezed into the cab. But no sooner had they got the message and started reversing than a second lorry shot round the corner and came bumping across the carpets to join them. More shrieks!

Pandemonium! but the party was a great success. The singers sang 'Happy Anniversary to You', the Parsee food was served in bubbling copper cauldrons, and we all sat out at round tables in the deliciously cool twilight. I sat next to a crusading feminist journalist. There is much to occupy her here. The Fundamentalist laws mean that a woman who conceives after rape can be stoned to death, because without four male witnesses, rape is not accepted by the courts. I also met Arabella, a tame turkey who lives in the shade of the necon tree, which looks rather like a ginkgo, grows ten feet a year if watered, and whose bark can be used for cleaning your teeth and keeping off mosquitoes. She was prudently slim.

March 2

Today's the day.

When I went out to swim this morning, I found the tent *covered* in dew. The weight of the water had pulled some of the stitching apart, leaving huge pools of water on the carpets. By lunchtime the piano still hadn't arrived, so I began to panic.

At last, at 4 p.m., it arrived in an open lorry with *seventeen* men of all ages, in bright turbans and unkempt beards, all clinging in or under or on top of the great instrument. On the lid, swinging his little legs, sat a very old man with a wrinkled brown face and black, black eyes, holding a musket, guarding the Goethe Institute's Steinway. As it was being unceremoniously unloaded, Bryan murmured in my ear, 'Would you lend your piano for this?'

John arrived.

'When is the piano tuner coming?' I asked.

'Unfortunately he has left Karachi for three days.'

Three days? We hadn't got three hours. Bryan tried it – not too bad – but then a very smart young man bustled in and proceeded to tune it to perfection.

Midnight.

Phew! A great performance by the four principals. There were 450 in the audience, fifteen rows deep but slightly raised. All four principals kept disappearing up the aisles to try to involve everyone in the ensembles. We couldn't hear any of them at the piano, but then they would miraculously reappear, still all together in perfect time. I honestly don't think you could find four other singers who could do it. I felt enormously proud of them. The audience were so beautiful – all swathed in multi-coloured silk and jewels, with huge dark eyes and rather Persian looks. I've never seen such a spectacular sight.

Afterwards we ate ravenously and Helen took me off to dance in the nightclub set up in the Consulate drawing-room. It's still going on, but I have to catch the early flight to Lahore.

March 4

I had a good flight up and was met by Tariq and Shahima Rehman. His father is an old friend of my mother's. We spent a happy morning visiting the great Fort, but by lunch I was feeling very ill. I went upstairs to my bathroom to splash some water on my face. Suddenly the floor tilted and reared up to smash me on the side of my head. I tried to grip the basin but slipped very slowly onto the cool marble tiles.

When I woke up I was on a drip, with an old nurse, very formally dressed in starched white, sitting knitting in the corner of my bedroom.

Somehow they had found me, put me to bed and called a doctor. Evidently I had a form of dysentery. The whole time in Karachi I had drunk, and brushed my teeth in, whisky – George had even refused to have a shower because of the warnings we had had.

My worst fear was this – if I was like this, what about the singers? Eventually I persuaded my hostess to telephone John. When she got through, the news was mixed. Noel and Helen were both in hospital, but the others had made the London flight with no apparent problem.

March 10

Back in London, still feeling very odd. I had flown back to
Karachi stuffed with tiny but effective pills, drinking lemonade
and salt. John's driver, Robin, met me to take me over to where
Noel and Helen were staying. They were very brave but very
pale, and will follow in a few days. Then I caught the London
flight. The air hostess took one look at the pills I was
swallowing and moved me to a secluded seat, watching me
intermittently with ill-concealed nervousness.

As soon as I got back, I rang George.

'So you got the flight?'

'Yes,' he said. 'But most of the passengers probably wished
we hadn't.'

No need to elaborate – it had been dreadful.

But now: *Figaro* and *Don Giovanni*.

March 12

We began on *Figaro* today with the overture. It's rather
unnerving when the new company gets together. There are
always more new faces than I expect. But lots of familiar ones as
well. Alice is in a smart green track suit, Helen looks stunning in
jeans and a simple white blouse. Caroline Friend is back – dark,
medium height, always smiling, with great poise. She has a little
daughter Rosamund who sometimes comes to rehearsals, but
she must be at school today. Blair and George are still suffering,
but Bryan is in relaxed confident form, as ever.

The morning was spent singing through the opera, first with
one cast, then with the other. Some are straight understudies;
others, like Alice and Caroline, are sharing the role, doing
perhaps fifteen performances each. *Figaro*, particularly, has sold
well. Our employers know their audiences will know of the
opera at least, but more probably already love it.

Amy looking rather pale today. She's understudying Barbarina. I saw Peter asking her something at lunch. She shook her head violently. When I got back for the afternoon session, Matt came up to say that Amy had gone home.

'Is she ill?'

'Yes,' he said. 'She says she's very sorry.'

'Any idea what's wrong?' I asked him.

He shook his head.

I'm starting in darkness, with the various men creeping back to their bedrooms from a night out – the Count first, confident and yawning, then Basilio (goodness knows where he's been, I've never been convinced by his half-hearted wooing of Marcellina), finally Cherubino, scuttling about, disturbed by the footmen (Colin and Bruce Carter resplendent in mulberry velvet) and hiding under the piano. Susanna comes in to check the Countess's breakfast, hears Cherubino (a chance for me to introduce a visual quote from Jean Renoir's *La Règle du Jeu* – she freezes in mid-motion up on her toes, like her opposite number Lisette when Octave calls for Madame's cloak in the film), and thus is already on stage for Figaro and their opening duet.

March 13

On, on we race. Timing in farce is all, particularly when the Italian doesn't exactly help out an English audience. 'Double-takes' are a matter of practice – the master of all time is Jimmy Finlayson, the moustachioed stooge in many of the best Laurel and Hardy films – for example, the bartender in *Way Out West*.

My sons Harry and Alexander are pretty good too (through copying him). George and Roberto don't find it so easy, and I am diffident of doing it myself. Nevertheless, we try, try, try, and it's getting better. This is the moment when the Count, describing how he had found Cherubino hiding under a carpet in another girl's bedroom, demonstrates by flicking aside the cover only to reveal – Cherubino again! It is inherently a good joke, but because the audience already know he is there, the joke has to be the Count's reaction rather than the *coup de théâtre* of finding someone unexpectedly. Which makes it a little more testing.

March 14

Noel and Helen are very devout, and occasionally we have prayer meetings when the company is under particular stress. The problem is that the stress is often concentrated among those who attend the prayers, breaking out again immediately afterwards.

This comes as no surprise to my mother.

'I've always noticed', she says, 'that the congregation in the church invariably contains the most cantankerous people in the village.'

Today there was nowhere quiet in the hall, so eight of us went to sit in my car – it's rather long, with three rows of seats if required. So in we clambered, I put on the heater and Helen led off with a prayer. She'd hardly started before there came a tapping. Noel wound down his window.

'Hello, Noel.' It was a singer from another company rehearsing upstairs. 'How's tricks?'

'Hello,' Noel replied. 'Look, I'll join you at the pub later. We're having a prayer meeting at the moment.' And he wound the window up. The singer paused for a moment, then walked slowly down the road. I was distracted by watching him in the wing mirror while Helen continued. He took some more steps, stopped, turned round, looked at us, and came back.

Tap, tap, tap.

Helen sighed and stopped again. Noel wound down his window.

'What is it?' he said testily.

'You are pulling my leg, aren't you?' asked the singer anxiously.

March 15

'Porgi Amor' – the Countess's entrance aria that opens Act 2. Very beautiful, very poignant, and very difficult to sing. I want to try to suggest someone suicidal with depression – lacking all confidence or will to go on fighting for her husband's love. After all, that's what she's actually saying to Eros. 'Please give him back, or let me die.'

I have seen it done ironically, with a smile (absurd), or as a dipsomaniac (ingenious); I did think of piling on the agony by having her pregnant (after all, she has a child by the Count before Cherubino's adulterous offspring – and we can see that Cherubino is not so far off success), but the designer protested so articulately that I abandoned the idea.

'Freddie?'

Anne Barclay had brought a picnic lunch to the rehearsal rooms. The others had all gone out, so she was playing Mendelssohn on the piano – 'A Song Without Words'.

'What?'

'What is Pavilion Opera trying to do?'

'Help!' I paused for thought. 'I suppose we're trying to present operas in a more realistic, more dynamic style. To make them more approachable and more emotionally moving. And trying to dispel the pompous image that opera has acquired this century. *And* to earn our living. That's enough to start with!'

She started to play again, something by Schubert, soft yet infinitely poignant. It was so peaceful sitting there listening to the music, surrounded by the gaudy clutter of rehearsal: a gilded chair, some sky-blue waistcoats and a scarlet cloak.

'Do you think people will go on employing you indefinitely?'

'Perhaps,' I said. 'I hope so. So long as we concentrate on helping them to make a profit out of their evening. *And* so long as we don't leave a series of smoking ruins to mark our progress.'

I TOLD YOU WE SHOULDN'T HAVE INVITED PAVILION OPERA BACK!

Bruce Rankin came back from lunch and picked up the book Anne had left on the piano.

'Proust?' he said. 'I've always meant to try him.'

'You MUST,' I butted in. 'It's *so* wonderful. But don't let anyone sell you the old Scott Moncrieff translation. The new one by Terence Kilmartin is *far* better. It's so *funny*, you see.'

'Thanks,' he said, moving away.

'Write it down,' I insisted. 'KILMARTIN.'

'Well,' he paused and smiled, 'actually I think I'd rather read it in the French.'

March 16

I like a bit of drama, just to keep the audience on their toes. So we set up a table with unbreakable items beside the Countess's settee. When her husband hears someone in her dressing room, he loses his temper, starts shouting and then throws over the table.

Our audiences seem to love family quarrels. So I'm giving her a spark as well. The more he rages, the more she holds her ground, even advances shouting at him, giving him a chance to retreat, show momentary loss of assurance, paving the way for his uncertain wooing of Susanna in Act 3. And when she kneels, asserting her innocence, and he curses her, I've asked Alice to fix him with her piercing blue eyes, and make them bulge slightly, like the woman on whom I'm basing this character. Alice was late this morning, so we are ill at ease with each other.

'Is that right?' she says, showing no emotion at all that I can see.

'No. No, it's not. I want you to look really angry.'

She tries again. Fails.

'Alice . . .' I go over and crouch beside her.

'Well, Fred-dee?' she glares at me.

'That's it! That's IT!' I'm over the moon.

'Look at him as if he's me,' I explain.

At least she smiles, and the next try is *excellent*!

March 17

Now it's Emma. She's been stumping about all day. When I asked her to try harder in the dance, she walked straight off the carpet and disappeared into the Ladies.

'Now what?' I asked in despair.

'Leave it to me, Freddie.' Enid ran after her.

'We'll take a fifteen-minute break,' I said to Bruce Carter.

As the others dispersed towards the kettles, Enid came back. 'She'll be all right, Freddie,' she said. 'She's just a bit upset.'

'Well, I'll be a bit upset if she doesn't get that dance right.'

'Don't be like that.' Enid has a lovely grin.

'All right,' I said. 'But try and persuade her to join us soon.'

I always have great difficulty with prolonged ensembles. The easiest thing is to go into some form of dance, which I absolutely hate. Not being able to read music, it is difficult for me to give accurate cues for personalized business. It's a question of instinct – every director's crucial stock-in-trade.

The *Figaro* Act 2 Finale is probably the most sophisticated climax ever written. It starts with a duet (Count and Countess) and gradually builds up with first Susanna, then Figaro, then Antonio and then the three conspirators, Marcellina, Basilio and Bartholo, all joining in the mêlée. This is the point when much repetitive singing leaves the cast with no obvious moves.

We all consult and come up with a spare but plausible pattern of group and individual movements that keeps the picture shifting. But from past experience, I know these last few bars will haunt me all year – reproaching me for not finding something more satisfactory. It's so much more difficult presenting it in the round. The only time I directed an opera for a large stage, it was refreshing to find how relatively easy it is to group characters and to plot a shifting process when it will only be judged from one side, and at a respectful distance!

Directing is both an exhilarating and a very lonely occupation. The first year we put on *Don Pasquale* (1982), we did twelve performances. At the end of the last, I said to the baritone, 'If I never hear that opera again, I really shan't mind!'

'Ah,' he said, 'that's because you're an amateur, Freddie. We professionals have a rather different approach.'

Ouch!

I suppose I remained an amateur until the 1985 débâcle. Bryan, Noel, Colin, Helen and I were all in Perthshire putting on *Don Pasquale* for the Dunkeld Festival when news began to percolate through that all was not going well in rehearsals at Thorpe Tilney.

'No girl should be asked to do what I'm doing,' moaned a soprano over a crackling line.

'For example?' I asked, angry at these interruptions. We were earning money. They were spending it.

'I-crackle-had to-crackle, crackle-and THEN-*crackle*! What do you think of THAT?'

'I can't really hear.'

'. . . crackle . . .'

'WAIT TILL I GET BACK!' I shouted. Our house telephone connection has always been intermittent.

I had great faith in the director, an experienced man with a nice sense of humour. He was in sole charge of both new productions. But we got back to find revolution in the air. So I summoned all the singers into the dining-room, stood up, and lectured them for twenty minutes on the professional imperative of co-operating with the director.

'It's the principle of the thing,' I announced grandiloquently. 'It's his job you threaten by undermining his authority. What if he got into the habit of saying that one or more of you were not singing properly? You sing. He directs.'

They listened to me in glum silence.

'Now,' I said cheerfully, 'let's run Act 1.'

Afterwards, I took the director into my study, paid his fee in full and put him in a car to take him to the station. We had five days until the first night. Various singers volunteered to contact directors they had worked with. But I knew I had to redirect the operas myself. There simply wasn't time for anything else. I knew the singers. I knew the operas. And we got on with it. But I had learned one valuable lesson: when I start talking grandly about principle, I must remember I shall probably have to eat my words within half an hour.

March 19

Lunch at school with Harry and Alexander, both working hard under considerable pressure. But they look healthy and confident and are looking forward to the holidays.

March 20

Amy's back, and looking stunning. Everyone's noticed the difference. After lunch we ran the opera with the understudies.

'Amy's rather a find,' I murmured to Bryan.

He smiled enigmatically.

'Don't you think?' I asked anxiously.

'Oh, yes,' he said. 'She's quite a handful.'

'Meaning?'

'You'll see,' he said, turning back to the piano.

Act 3 of *Figaro* is a feast of beautiful music. The opening duet between the Count and Susanna, where she gets confused and pretends to succumb to him, is my favourite moment in the opera. I've been playing it over and over again in the car. Then (because we slightly change the order) come the two grand arias, with the Count, his pride injured by realizing it's all a trick, swearing vengeance against Figaro, followed by the Countess, changing into rather more optimistic mood. She also complains about her maid, Susanna, getting what she wants herself. The Count is often played as a domineering employer, the Countess rarely. And then the 'discovery' sextet, where Figaro finds out that Bartolo and Marcellina are his parents! And the finale, with the Count's ominous promise: 'You will see how I reward those who are dear to me.'

March 21

A day off while Terry took more choreography and I flew to Paris for the day to look for a suitable room. It was also the day of the photo-calls for the programme at Osterley, so I explained it all to Jo Young, our eager American publicity agent, and left them to it.

March 22

Two horrors!

I make detailed notes on the score to help me direct the cast. It's quite a vulnerable job, and one becomes perfectly paranoid – translating every snigger or murmur off-stage into criticism of what one is doing. At least, I do, and I've observed our other producers reacting in the same way. These notes give me a little extra confidence.

The fourth act is the most difficult one, especially in the round. Stage directions call for Cherubino to kiss the Count instead of the Countess (by *mistake*), for the Count to slap Figaro instead of Cherubino (because he too gets in the way), and for the Count to woo the Countess, believing her to be Susanna – and all this while retaining their credibility as well as the audience's credulity. *Plus* the extra music, needed to get people across a large stage, but providing its own built-in problems for characters in a small space. I opened my Act 4 folder to find it . . . BLANK! I suppose I'd planned to write it all down during my last two days on holiday. So – it's a question of improvising calmly.

This is not made any easier by the second horror.

Osterley, through the endlessly helpful and efficient Marilyn Scott, a tiny powerhouse at the V & A, is one of our most regular employers, three or four consecutive nights a year, unparalleled luxury for us.

The first year was a bit nervewracking. They had put the

piano in the wrong place, and the guards said it couldn't be moved. I got there early, found Marilyn there by chance and she over-ruled the (then) extremely surly manager.

Next, there was the question of moving the thing. There were three guards, in peaked caps, standing in the doorway. Determined not to be browbeaten, I got hold of the keyboard end myself and heaved. Nothing. Then I tried pushing. It wouldn't budge. Marilyn came in. She's really not very tall, but she immediately offered to help.

'No, no,' I said. 'Thank you. But no. However . . .' I added, glancing at the three giants watching us.

'Oh, dear me, no,' she said. 'Those are *uniformed* men.'

So that's the secret! Get a uniform and have a quiet life.

Well – things have changed since then. Year after year we went back, gradually making friends with all the staff. Many of them have changed, but some are still there, and it's so nice now to exchange smiles, shake hands and reflect on changing relationships.

Anyway – the point of this rigmarole is that now Marilyn allows us to take our publicity shots in Osterley. I had planned each shot and explained it all to Jo. When she came in, I asked her how it had gone.

'Fine. No problems,' she said. 'Although your picture of Blair and Alice caused quite a furore.'

'Really?' I had wanted Alice in a nightdress in front of the State Bed, with Blair wearing a turban peeping round the door. The rest of his costume wasn't ready, so I had said, 'Just have his head and the turban, nothing else.'

Would *you* have translated that into making him take off all his clothes, so that he was photographed stark naked, watched by the astonished guards, and the even more astonished National Trust visitors?

'What?' I yelled. 'Nothing on at ALL?'

'Oh, yeah,' she said. 'He had the turban on his head.'

I shall have to ring Marilyn. They'll probably cancel the contract.

March 23

One's worst fears are rarely fulfilled. Marilyn was charm itself, hadn't had a report, and presumed that everyone had taken it in good part.

Act 4 worked much better than ever before. Perhaps my notes have been a hindrance, holding back improvisation instead of forming a solid bedrock on which to build. Anyway, the opera is now complete. A week of run-throughs, and the dress rehearsal will be upon us.

I was rather surprised to see Emma leaving arm in arm with Ron, the new chorus baritone who never knows his lines. She was laughing animatedly. I looked anxiously across to where Peter was copying down details from the notice board, with Susan and Amy. If there's one thing I dread, it's an emotional bust-up. All seemed calm.

The vegetarians this year are playing up. Nicky Whitsun-Jones is a genuine one – and I will fight the world to keep her in tomato omelettes. But some of the others . . .

Yesterday Bruce Carter put up a list which simply asks for the names of those wanting vegetarian meals on tour. Bryan and I always sign so that there is enough. We then eat whichever is easier. Amy has signed, and Ron and Colin. But Otto's signature is followed by the words: 'Nothing fried or boiled, and *no* (underlined) mushrooms', whereas Emma has put 'Boiled is fine, but no processed cheese'.

March 27

My father died in hospital two days ago. I had to drive down to Basingstoke to identify him formally. He was scarcely recognizable, looking so much older. Some nonsense is written about Alzheimer's Disease. It is less of a burden for those who suffer from it than for those who look after them. He was never remotely aware of his increasing eccentricity, just becoming quieter and slower, though utterly unpredictable. He was still shooting regularly up to four months ago, to the unconcealed terror of his neighbours. In fact, the only person he ever shot (me) was in his sporting heyday, overwhelmed by a covey of grouse on his beloved Fence Butt on the return drive at Badachurn. As the illness developed, he was shadowed by a team of cheerful nurses whom he used to amuse at night by bursting out of his bedroom with his shotgun. My mother had quietly removed the firing pins, remembering no doubt our Scottish neighbour, Colonel Haig, who stalked and shot his butler.

When they couldn't stand the strain any longer, he went into a local nursing home, still eating well, and calm, though confused. It was a terrible strain for my mother, but, I repeat, for him a painless and unharassing end to an idyllic life. Helen, whom he greatly admired, has agreed to sing at his memorial service.

March 29

A moment's break in rehearsals while we dash up the M1 to perform at Kedleston in Derbyshire. It is a superbly confident building, a great square block with a massive portico surrounded by statues and flanked by two equally grand wings – James Paine this (the masculine) side, Robert Adam the other (feminine), garden front. Even the statues have haughty expressions. I don't think there'd have been many survivors here if we'd had an English Revolution to match the French. But it's a peaceful spot now for a quiet walk.

The Curzons have retreated to a wing, but obviously love the house and are typically relaxed about its treasures. The room I really wanted to do the opera in had the famous dolphin sofas, perhaps the grandest of all English-made furniture.

'Oh, please not!' said Lord Scarsdale. 'Whole chunks fell off

"*Thank God you're not vegetarian!*"

when they went to Washington. I couldn't bear to move them again.'

In any case, the National Trust are now in command, so that was out. Sadly the two greatest rooms, the Rotunda and the ineffably dignified Roman Hall, were out too, because of the acoustics. A bit of marble rather adds to the general tone. But rooms of *solid* marble? Deafening and blurred. They'd be marvellous for string quartets, or a harpsichord – but a full-blown Verdi ensemble would drive the audience screaming out into the night.

March 30

The *Figaro* dress rehearsal was awful. The audience never even smiled. They clapped politely at the end but the atmosphere of gloom weighed heavily on the cast, and also on me. I'm afraid I may have let them down. There's a month before the first night. I don't want to change anything, but it looks as if my interpretation is at odds with what this audience (mainly friends and relations of the cast) would have hoped for.

But perhaps I am over-reacting. I am always more relaxed at dress rehearsals like this when Christopher Cowell has been the designer. I can't always afford to use him, and we do have our ups and downs, but professionally he is in a class of his own. His lavish designs are exquisitely drawn and coloured, and the costumes themselves accurately reflect the designs and are finished by him personally with painstaking care. So I can enjoy his skill, and save my worries for the bank manager. What's more, he always makes me laugh. His wit has that peculiarly French mordancy, perhaps a reflection of the fact that he was born in Paris. One minute we are at one another's throats, the next he has made me laugh so much that I have forgotten whatever we were disputing.

April 3

Off to Venice with Harry and Alexander and some friends. Harry is studying History of Art, so this is a wonderful opportunity to have fun *and* promote his education! There are three adults and seven children, so we should be able to keep each other busy and amused.

April 9

England again, and I take it all back about comptrollers. Today I drove up to Chatsworth to plan for a performance. Mr Oliver, their Comptroller, is a quiet man of great charm and efficiency. We measured out the Painted Hall, smothered in Roman extravaganzas by Laguerre; as if that wasn't enough, the spare panels are filled with glowing flowers by Monnoyer. Then we sorted out a dressing room (the Mary Queen of Scots apartment). Next, because he could see I was interested, he took me off to see the chapel with its famous alabaster altarpiece. Typically dotty was one corridor filled by a long dark boat – the barque in which one of the Dukes had negotiated the Bosphorus. After that, a look at the model of the house (to explain the incorporation of the original sixteenth-century structure) and at the topographical landscapes illustrating the changing architecture of the façades.

'It's a nice place to work,' he said. 'They're a lovely family to work for.' Who could hope for more?

I got back in time for the last half hour of rehearsal. Bryan came to White's with me for dinner.

'I've been reading this fascinating book on psychotherapy,' I told him. 'It's frightfully interesting. It says that when people say they've got a problem, it's probably not the real one, but just a smokescreen for some other problem that they can't face up to.'

'Well, of course,' he said. 'That's just what you'd expect.'

'Oh?' He's so sensible. 'Anyway,' I went on, 'it'll be a great help for dealing with everyone's problems on tour.'

'Maybe even your own?' he murmured.

April 10

Golly. Day one of rehearsals for *Don Giovanni*. I like to begin as I mean to go on. Last year my mother gave me a huge laundry basket to store the boots and shoes. We know the Don has to get into the Commendatore's house somehow. So I'm starting with an old woman lugging in the laundry basket, helped by a gormless maid. The maid (a stage manager) slopes off, leaving the old woman slumped on the basket. Is the coast clear? It is. The 'woman' flings off her rags – it is Leporello in disguise. Open the basket, out comes the Don, masked and be-daggered. Let Rapine and Murder commence!

When he comes back, it is with Donna Anna entwined round him, trying to pull his trousers off. Is she in full evening dress? Or a tightly-laced bodice? Well, is it *likely*? He woke her up in her own bed, and her later reminiscences tell us most of what ensued. So what is she in? A towel? Too small. Nothing at all? Too obvious . . . A decorous sheet, designed to slip, sounds just right. The designer groaned when I asked for this. But he

promised to produce it next week, as we shall need to rehearse in it regularly to find out the problems now rather than later.

As for the Commendatore's murder, the duel is always so dull. We know from Tirso de Molina's play that the Don is the son of the Commendatore's friend, and indeed they are at Court together. So what if he pulls the Don's mask off? First the old man will think it is all a joke. But the Don will have to kill him. Treacherously. That way we will establish from the start that he is wholly without scruples. Attractive? Sexy? Oh, yes, but a real scoundrel. And never, never to be trusted.

April 11

The advent of the Friends of Pavilion Opera has been a good thing. It gives us a data-base of people who support us and I hope joining encourages them to feel part of the team. They pay us £15 or more a year; we give them a concert, a free programme, access to rehearsals, seasonal newsletters and help with bookings. But there can be misunderstandings, like today.

Anne Barclay was meeting me for dinner. She had lost my telephone number and rang Christine at Thorpe Tilney.

ANNE: 'Have you got Freddie's number?'
CHRISTINE: 'Are you a Friend?'
ANNE (*taken aback*): 'Yes – I *think* so.'
CHRISTINE: 'Either you are or you aren't.'
ANNE (*thinking hard*): 'Well, I do like him . . .'
CHRISTINE (*searching the files*): 'You're not on *my* list.'

And so on.

April 12

Today we started on the Zerlina–Masetto scene. I was still seething over Ron not knowing his lines. It couldn't be clearer in the contract. They are all REQUIRED to know both words and music from Day One.

I started with Enid and Philip and we got right through to the Don's seduction duet. It went really well, and Philip caught the right mood of rebellion mixed with fear. There were quite a lot of unfamiliar faces around, but I was gradually setting names to them.

We broke off for coffee and then repeated it with the understudies. Anne Gerbic I knew was reliable, but I wasn't sure about Philip's cover.

'Come on, you two. Let's try that scene again from the start.'

Anne and the earnest young man beside her came into the middle, obediently, he carrying the score. I signalled to Bryan to start playing, and Anne sailed into her piece. The other man just stayed staring at his score. He looked up and smiled.

'Don't you know the part?'

'Not really.'

'Well, do you think you could possibly act it?' I said rather acidly.

'I'll try.' His smile was of more value than his homework, it seemed. So we struggled through. He danced well, had obviously been following the action, but hardly sang at all. I was beginning to lose my temper.

The Don was about to come on, several people were watching now. This is such a bad example to everyone, I thought. No one will try.

'Do you know any of the music?'

He shook his head. 'I'm afraid not.'

Noel, who co-ordinates the casting, was standing by the notice board. Slamming down my score, I went across to him.

'This is an absolute disgrace. What the bloody hell am I paying this man for? The contract couldn't be more precise.'

'What's the matter?' He had only just arrived.

'That bloody understudy. He's done no preparation at all.'

'Where?'

'There!' I said, pointing at the man with the misplaced smile.

'But Freddie, that's not Masetto,' said Noel. 'That's Rupert, the new singing coach.'

Oh dear.

April 15

I'm not often to be found among the Great and the Good. Indeed, I have a marked preference for the slim and naughty. However, tonight I went to dine with friends after the rehearsals, and who should I meet but (forgive the name-dropping) the Chairman of Covent Garden. There were the usual jokes about the two extremes (fair enough), and about my singers subsidizing his through their income tax (even fairer). When we had a moment alone, I plucked up courage and accosted him.

'What really interests me is this,' I said. 'When you've got the Covent Garden Board all sitting round a table, suppose you took away the label saying "Royal Opera", and put one in its place saying "Marks & Spencer". Would you really all talk in the same sort of way, spending irrespective of income and looking to the Government to bail you out by raising taxes?'

'That's totally simplistic,' he said. 'It has no relevance at all.' He started to move away, staring into his glass.

'You really don't see it,' I said, half to myself.

He came back.

'What is the largest number of people *you* have ever had on a stage?' he asked.

Well, thank God for Versailles, I thought (our only major expedition). 'Thirty-three.' (Well – it was twice as good as seventeen, our usual maximum.)

'There you are.' He walked away triumphantly, and yet I didn't think his point was proved. Of course, if you have a huge stage to fill, and have a problem about trying to reach the ears at the back of a giant theatre, a large chorus (at, say, £200 a week each) is as cheap a way as any. But it doesn't explain the extraordinary profligacy of competent men and women, no doubt able to balance a budget at home or in their jobs, coolly spending the nation's tax returns on these evenings. I put it down to lack of confidence.

April 16

If ever there's a finale that causes trouble, it's the end of *Don Giovanni*, Act 1. One minute the Don is surrounded by his enemies, vainly threatening to kill Leporello as if he were the real villain; the next, he's free. In between there are a great many bars of rousing, furious chorus. Sometimes there's no explanation, sometimes it's 'with one bound, he was free'; I've even seen it done in 'suspended time', when the characters freeze – a dramatic device as over-used as that creaking old cliché of a group of people coming on stage and deciding to stage an opera (or a play).

My solution seems more fun – a proper Prisoner of Zenda sword-fight. But, at such close range, it has to seem *real*. Real swords, real speed – the spirit of Douglas Fairbanks (or, more particularly, Basil Rathbone in *The Court Jester*). I was lucky to find a first-class expert to stagemanage the fighting: Wolf Christian, known in the company as Conan the Barbarian because of his towering height and immense breadth. Next I had to square the insurers (remember, we've only got twelve feet of width). Today we started. Just fencing to begin with. Then, fencing getting up and down on tables and chairs. Then speeding it up. I made the understudies join me sitting in the front rows while this was going on. It seemed terrifyingly dangerous.

'That was too close!' someone shouted.

'We'll have to shorten the swords,' suggested Bruce Carter.

This made quite a difference. I also privately had all the houses concerned alerted to our need for fourteen feet of width for this one show, for safety reasons. The singers found it very exhausting. We reduced it to Don Giovanni versus Don Ottavio, with Masetto intervening at the end when it looks as though Don Giovanni will kill his opponent. Laughing, he disarms them both and runs through the cowering crowd. It looks as if they will have something to cower about.

Rehearsing the sword fight.

'This is my husband, Freddie.' I was just leaving when Amy grabbed my arm and led me to the squat, silent sentry we had all become accustomed to, at his post in the shadows beyond the swing door.

'This is Raoul.'

'How do you do,' I said, with suitable enthusiasm. He took my hand with an anxious smile.

'She's a great addition to the team,' I said. 'She's doing a wonderful job.'

'Raoul loves the production,' she said. This very welcome compliment would have had more force if he had ever shown any sign of looking inside our sanctum.

'Oh, good,' I said. 'I hope you're coming to the dress rehearsal.'

'I'm afraid I shall be busy that day,' he said abruptly.

It was a low voice, rather clouded and with an indefinable accent. 'Where on earth did she find him?' I asked Bryan.

'At the college. They were students together.'

'Does he sing?'

'Not so as you'd notice.'

'He has a face like a toad,' I said.

'Yes.'

'Freddie! Can you come and look at this costume'. It was Colin. This year's Count, Roberto, is rather larger than his predecessor.

'Is that acceptable?' he asked, indicating the constricted figure.

'No,' I said, reluctantly. 'We'll need a new one.'

Money, money, money.

April 17

I tried today to introduce my favourite gag from the *Court Jester* duel.

Danny Kaye has been hypnotized into being a brilliant

swordsman, better even than Basil Rathbone. But there's a flaw. The snap of a finger turns him back into a bumbling fool. As you can imagine, there is much snapping of fingers, changing him from one mode to the other. But while he is the great virtuoso, he slashes his sword at a candelabra, apparently missing all the candles.

Basil Rathbone laughs. 'Ha-Ha!'

Danny Kaye, with magnificent nonchalance, blows at the candles, and they all fall over, sliced cleanly in half. *Cut* to Rathbone's face, showing consternation.

We tried hard: we sawed the candles in half, we stuck them back on with just a little glue. But it simply didn't work. The more we rehearsed it, the lower the temperature in the room fell. By the end, I didn't even think it funny myself. So we reverted to undiluted blood and thunder. Great relief all round.

April 19

Nearly late for rehearsals. When I arrived, several people studiously examined their watches.

On to Act 2. I still haven't thought how to solve the graveyard scene, but we're feeling our way towards it, trying to make the story work despite the rather odd conjunction of some of the scenes. There's one point where in most modern versions you get three major arias in succession, so I decided to cut one; the one which didn't sound too good, if I'm being totally truthful. The overall result will be better, but I'm afraid it is *not* a good decision, and will no doubt cause complaints. I don't think I can really base it on the undeniable truth that Mozart changed his operas all the time in performance, substituting new arias for different singers. Be that as it may, audiences are accustomed to hear the lot (apart from the Act 2 Zerlina–Leporello duet, which I have never heard performed).

There is a theory that *Don Giovanni* was originally intended to have four acts (like *Figaro*), with the Act 2 sextet (the unmasking of Leporello) as its Act 3 finale. It does sound rather like a finale. The idea is that Mozart ran out of time, and had to do the best he could. It's usually asserted that he wrote the overture on the night before the first performance; if so, his orchestra must have been pretty good. Or maybe audiences had lower expectations, then. Performing *Zauberflöte* six nights a week must have been quite a strain on some of the voices.

April 20

Another puzzle in this opera is the chorus. What was wrong with the choruses available to Mozart in Vienna and Prague that he gave them so little to do? One can quite see that they weren't especially necessary in *Seraglio* and *Così*. But *Figaro*? And here, in *Don Giovanni*? Just thirty-eight bars in a whole opera? They must have been pretty dire.

But I've found a solution for the graveyard scene. In our first-ever production, Patrick Garland had singers dressed as graveyard effigies gliding on through mist to take up various positions on stage. This worked spectacularly well on the stage at Derngate and Chichester – but not on the carpet, where the difficulties with smoke, and the *sound* of their progress, produced chuckles rather than fear.

So this time we'll do it in complete darkness. Bruce has rigged up two lanterns with their lights shining out of only one shutter. Held at the right angle, with Bryan's piano light turned down low, the only things visible are two disembodied faces, Leporello and then Don Giovanni, floating in the darkness. It's impossible to get the proper impression in a daylight rehearsal, but I believe it will work.

April 21

And now to the supper scene. I try to avoid props, knowing the problems of transporting them, especially abroad. And *Don Giovanni* has outsold all my expectations: forty-five nights so far, including three nights in France, as well as Jersey and America: the most we've ever given for an individual show. I've had to recruit three Donna Annas to take the strain.

This supper is the climax of the story – the *ne plus ultra* of Hammer House of Horrors in opera. One minute the Don is gorging on wine, women and pheasant, the next he's being dragged down to Hell by a refrigerated spectre from the past.

So – a table groaning with food, a guttering rococo candelabra smothered in dripping candlewax (thank heavens for those splendidly over-the-top shops on either side of Kensington Church Street catering for who–knowns–what crazy designers) and, above all, an effective smoke machine.

Chris Cowell, our very articulate and very funny designer, who arrived as part of the *Traviata* package in 1984, has come up with a brilliant design for the Commendatore – a sort of mouldering shroud, the face blotched and distorted by the sort of stocking you'd wear if you had designs on a High Street bank. And gushing from between his ribs, a hideously stained scarlet mass of linen.

Most of the act is pretty plain sailing. But the end is obviously difficult. How do you get the Don off without the audience laughing? My original idea was to set up a red searchlight outside the door. When that heart–stopping music announces the statue's (or ghost's) entrance, the stage lights flicker and fail, leaving only the candelabra. Red light floods under the door, along with the first of the smoke. Leporello bursts through – there is a violent flash of red, looming smoke – he slams the door. But then it opens, and through the billowing red smoke emerges . . . a voice. Nothing more. And Don Giovanni is mesmerized at last into following it. I still think we might add in the red light when we come to revive it. But this time I settled for Chris's creepy figure and smoke. And as the act ends, the ghost withdraws to the door, throwing out a single arm which invisibly checks the Don, several feet away. Struggling to get free, yet actually pushing himself backwards along the carpet, Don Giovanni is drawn inexorably towards the motionless figure of his Doom. Then, just when they are both by the door, the ghost pounces (like Old Brown the owl in *The Tale of Squirrel Nutkin*) and drags his victim to eternal damnation.

And if the audience dare to applaud after that, I will go back to farming. I want them silenced by the pervasive presence of fear.

Should we include the final ensemble or not? Mozart couldn't decide, and did it one night with, the next without.

Bryan and I have talked about it endlessly. It's a beautiful passage, but you lose the thunderous climax of Don Giovanni's final yell, cunningly reinforced by Leporello under the table.

In the end, we decided to do it – it gives the audience time to recover, and implants a nice eighteenth-century feel with the mixture of moralizing and pragmatism – the grandees congratulating themselves on the end of a sinner, while the servants go off to have a drink and seek new employment. A great opera to work on.

April 25

The *Don Giovanni* dress rehearsal.

We were delayed in starting because both Peter and Amy were late getting into costume. They were both flushed from running when they came in.

'Sorry we're late.'

'That's OK,' I said. 'But try to be quick. The others are all ready.'

They hurried off to Colin's room.

'Bryan?'

'Yes, Freddie?'

'Peter lives in Ealing, doesn't he?'

'Yes.'

'And Amy lives in Kent?'

'Yes, Freddie.'

'Do you think . . .'

He smiled. 'It's not like you to be so slow,' he said.

Oh? Well, it's none of my business.

The dress rehearsal itself was not bad. Certainly the audience liked it, although there were one or two serious shortfalls which need ironing out. Chris's costumes are splendidly vivid – whatever else anyone says, they can't call it drab. Don Giovanni in scarlet and gold, Donna Anna in blue and then purple, with swirling hats only outdone by Elvira's Act 1 creation (to disguise her for the beginning when her husband doesn't recognize her at first).

One unscheduled moment. At the end of Leporello's catalogue aria, listing the Don's conquests, he (Noel) goes up to several members of the audience to confide, 'You know what it's like'. One of those he chose was a member of the company not noted for his interest in women, who very slowly and very sadly shook his head. The rest of the company burst out laughing. Goodness knows what the other members of the audience made of this.

There's a dangerous glamour about the role of Don Giovanni which *does* something for a man. Whatever success Roberto may have as himself, he evidently becomes irresistible as the Don. Three of the girls in the audience delayed our post mortem by insisting on being introduced to him afterwards – unheard of in a dress rehearsal.

April 28

A very good first night at the Haberdashers' Hall. The sword fight worked perfectly; the audience were galvanized by the clash of flashing steel, and the first act ended with great *éclat*. The cemetery scene would have worked if Noel and Roberto had held their lanterns straight, but in the event they kept letting them droop, lighting here and there a dim face in the audience. That can soon be put right.

The smoke machine was a sensation. We were lucky to have a little lobby, enclosed by two doors, one opening into the performance room, the other into a kitchen corridor. Alan stood in this space and Bruce filled it from the corridor with smoke, so when Alan opened the door, a great billow of silent smoke belched into the room, engulfing the audience on that side. I had a brief glimpse of a woman flapping angrily with her programme before she disappeared completely from view. And then – yes – through the swirling cloud, very slowly, emerged this petrifying creature; first we saw his distorted head, then the indistinct torso – it was splendidly creepy.

Afterwards, we all joined up for champagne and smoked salmon: a highly enjoyable evening.

April 29

Live performances produce electrifying tension. Will a singer fall ill at the last moment? Or have a car crash on the way? Will the understudy be near the telephone? Will our employer have an attack of nerves?

I suppose this is why it is so exciting. When you add this nightly charge to its opposite, the soothing effect of beautiful music, you are plunged into a very heady cocktail of emotions.

Perhaps the most heart-stopping anticipation comes from waiting for the high notes: the Duke's in *Rigoletto*, or the Queen

THE TOP NOTE

of the Night's in *The Magic Flute*. Will they make it?

They always do, but the tension before builds up as the music draws us inexorably towards the moment of truth.

The trouble is that some arias have been modified by popular artists in the past, who have embroidered what is written to suit their own capacities. My *bête noire* is the high note at the end of Ernesto's Act 2 aria in *Don Pasquale*. It's a wonderful opera, far too seldom performed – no doubt because of the difficulty in casting Ernesto, a role that calls for sustained singing in the top register. It was our second opera, and we have done performances in all sorts of unlikely places because it is so popular with our employers: it's short, it's funny, and it's full of good tunes. And when the wife turns on her husband, delighted smiles break out through the whole audience.

Donizetti, in his wisdom, wrote a low note to complete this double aria. Somewhere along the line someone with a secure top C decided to give it his best shot, and ever since tenors believe they have a duty to oblige. And it rarely works. After two years of this, I took to INSTRUCTING our Ernestos (a heroic band anyway) to stick to the score. One by one, they would nod, looking rather affronted. And then, once the Ernesto of the evening was out in front of the audience and thus beyond my immediate control, I would see a dogged expression creeping over his face.

'If Caruso could do it, I can!'

And the next thing we know, it's 'Cerchero . . . AYEE'. An awful sound, but the audience usually applaud, because they think it's kind.

The worst was in Cambridgeshire. We had an Ernesto who was rather crazed at the best of times. That night he chanced to watch a horror film on our host's television set just before the show. His eyes were bloodshot, and I knew we were in for a rough night. Strangely enough, Act 1 was perfect. But his eyes were still red, and unnaturally fixed. Off went the previous singers and Act 2 began. Ernesto started in and slammed down his suitcase (he's about to emigrate to escape his disappointed love).

Well, he fairly drowned the piano with both arias, giving them really strong treatment. The audience were enthralled, but Bryan and I knew what to expect. We exchanged anxious glances; I crossed the fingers of both hands, fixed him with a furious stare, and willed him to sing the low note, the note that is actually written. He was purple in the face by this time. As the second aria winds up, the piano takes over, and then the climax. He swelled his chest, cast a defiant look at me and let out a piercing, ear-shattering howl. The audience looked stunned, and then clapped loudly. Method acting meets Pavilion Opera? It was strangely moving, but it wasn't music.

'That was an interesting note,' I said afterwards.

'Freddie,' he said, staring into my eyes. 'I give you my solemn promise.'

'Oh, good,' I said. 'You'll stick to the score?'

'Eh?' He looked surprised. 'No – I'll never ever watch television before a show again.'

Luckily, these days, Bruce and Blair have too much respect for Donizetti to tinker with his masterpiece.

April 30

Rigoletto at Worthington, home of Bill and Anthea Runceman; a broad, solid lump of eighteenth–century masonry, anchored by its two flanking courtyards and entered up a curving staircase of uncertain safety.

'I hate these stairs,' muttered Bruce Carter as we all staggered up with the carpet. Nicky Whitsun-Jones is ill, so it's a chance for me to remember quite how heavy our carpet really is.

Because it's a Saturday, I'm staying over the weekend. 'Who else is staying?' I asked, as Anthea showed me into a tall room with scarlet walls and green velvet curtains.

'Melissa Wyndham, George and Jane Holinshed, James and Caroline Knox – um – the Brents I think – and Bill's brother. One or two others – I just can't think. *Look* at this table. It's *smothered* in dust.'

Downstairs I could hear the piano tuner at work. Outside, the park stretched down to the river on one side, and up to a dense wood on the other. The room smelt deliciously of freesias. A large vase presided over the dressing table, and there was another small one on the bedside table. No books – but I'd brought my own.

I found my way back down the staircase and walked into the crowded Library. The first person I saw was Anne Barclay.

I'm never good at entering rooms full of people. It's a distinctly threatening experience at the best of times. But, *à la guerre comme à la guerre*. So I marched over, took her in my arms, and kissed her on both cheeks.

'How lovely to see you.' She looked pretty, but hunted.

'Tony!' I said, beaming expansively at her husband. Should I shake his hand? I decided not. He made no move either – and creased his eyes into triangular slices of ill-will.

'This is a great compliment,' I said breezily. 'I thought you hated opera.' Before he could reply, Anthea whisked me round the others.

Worthington Wooshouse.

Melissa was sitting by the fire. She gave a piercing shriek when she saw me.

'How are those boys? I just love Harry. Have you met Freddie's son Harry?' she asked a dark man who had been standing beside her. He was rubbing his ear and leant forward to shake my hand.

'No, I haven't had that pleasure,' he said gravely.

'Freddie is the Diaghilev of the Fens,' she told him.

'*Really*!' he said, unsuitably impressed.

I shook my head vigorously. 'Ignore Mel,' I said. 'You must judge us by what you see tonight.'

'I shall,' he said.

'You're wanted.' This from Bill, and indeed there was Colin in the doorway. There was a message that Rigoletto had an infection. His understudy was on the way. And could I talk to Matt about the lighting?

Downstairs I found Bruce Rankin warming up his voice for the Duke. I suddenly had an idea.

'Bruce!' I said, taking him by the arm.

'Freddie!' he responded.

'"Questa o quella".'

'Yes?' This is the Duke's first big aria, a swaggering bravura piece demanding the freedom to flirt with anyone, despite jealous husbands. If Tony was going to embarrass Anne wherever she went, I, as one of her friends, could at least join in on her side.

'If I point out the people concerned, will you sing the first

132

verse at a girl in the audience, and the second at her husband?'

'Will he attack me?'

'Of course not,' I laughed. I wasn't that sure. However . . . 'We'll wait till I see where they're sitting.'

'This is just a joke, isn't it?'

'Yes, Bruce,' I reassured him. 'It's just a joke.'

By seven the house was in a hubbub – laughter, shouting and the occasional practice notes ricocheting round the corridors and hallways. Bruce Carter and Matt were in uniform, selling the programmes, and the Duke's throne on its violet velvet dais looked magnificent in Bill's white and gold drawing-room.

It went rather well. Anne was placed in the front row, in the seats reserved for the house party. She had George Holinshed next to her on one side, Tony on the other. Since George is slight and wan, and Tony is big and red and fat, there was no danger of Bruce getting them muddled. Anyway, he's met Anne at rehearsals.

I dimmed the house lights and Bryan started playing the overture, which, in my production, is used to illustrate the Duke's power of life and death over his subjects, with one of the chorus temporarily playing the part of a masked hangman. Tonight he looked splendidly menacing, his bare chest gleaming with oil and the great noose swinging from his shoulder.

Up come the stage lights, on come the courtiers, the Duchess settles down to a game of cards and Bruce, as Duke, uncoils himself from his throne as the aria's first notes raise the audience's hopes. As usual he began by surveying the crowd, lip curled, eyes haughty – the very picture of a jaded, sadistic monarch.

Then his glance seemed to be caught by Anne's tense face. She has a warm natural complexion and wide brooding eyes. As he advanced towards her she snapped me a brief glance of panic before being engulfed in the burst of music from Bruce's majestic voice. She turned a glorious crimson and sat there entranced as he poured out Verdi's glittering notes, his eyes burning with passion.

As planned, the Duchess jumps up at the end of the first verse, flings down her cards, throws over her chair and runs past the Duke and his new inamorata, pausing only to give a scornful lift of her chin at whichever member of the audience has found herself in this unexpected part. The Duchess is Nicky Jackson, and she does it superbly. Tonight her stage scorn for Anne was palpable. The Duke laughs, the courtiers giggle, and immediately we're into the second verse: 'I scorn jealous husbands – they cannot prevail against my power.' When the Duke turned his attention a matter of a few inches and laughed in Tony's face, I thought for a terrible moment he was going to have a seizure. And suddenly I felt dreadfully penitent. What right had I to parade their private difficulties in such an irresponsibly malicious way? I was nothing to Anne except an affectionate friend – why humiliate her husband in this way? I longed for the aria to end. And it did. Bruce hit the final note with expansive gusto, turned, and gave me a ten second pop-eyed look of apprehensive warning. Anne was applauding loudly and Tony seemed to be holding her arm.

In the interval I had to organize some extra drinks for the cast, so the audience were beginning to move back to their seats when I joined them. I saw Anne by the fireplace.

'I loved the Duke's attentions,' she said, looking at me gravely.

'Wasn't it too obvious?' I asked.

'No,' she said. 'It was fun. And it very successfully demonstrates the point of the opera. His ability to dominate women. If Countess Ceprano hadn't gone next door with him, I certainly should have done.'

Oh?

At dinner, after the guests and the opera had departed, I had Melissa on one side, Jane Holinshed on the other. Melissa is on everyone's list for the best-dressed woman in London. She almost seems deliberately constructed to flatter couturiers with her svelte figure and glowing black hair. We gossiped through two courses until Anthea rapped on the table, her signal to make us change and talk to our other neighbour.

Jane Holinshed has a drawn beauty that I find deeply moving. I would give anything to be able to capture on canvas her haunting allure.

'So?' I said. 'What's up?' I knew that she had been having an affair with Ginger Alec-Smith, notoriously not a route to happiness.

'Do you know Ginger Alec-Smith?' she asked with an inconsequential air, playing with the stem of her wineglass.

'Jane!' I said. 'You may think that I still live in the Outer Hebrides. But yes, I have heard of your generosity in that direction.'

She looked pained.

'It was awful,' she said softly, after a pause.

'Well, honestly,' I said. 'Even I could have told you that. How long's it been going on?'

'It's over now,' she said. 'He's a very complicated character, you know.'

'Really?' I wasn't *that* interested.

'He's very much in thrall to his wife.'

'Perpetual strayers usually are.'

'George isn't!' We both laughed. George, across the table, was deeply absorbed in Caroline Knox, gazing into her eyes while tracing patterns on the table in front of her. She caught our glance and winked.

'I *knew* it was a mistake with Ginger,' she went on in a low voice. 'I just *knew* it, the very first time.'

'Well, why didn't you stop. It's been a long time, hasn't it?'

'Four Years,' she said portentously, under her breath.

'FOUR YEARS!' I said out loud.

'Don't shout it out. We all know Melissa is Radio London personified.'

'You're wrong there,' I said. 'She's very discreet about friends. But Jane! *Four years.*'

'I know. But I couldn't bear to hurt him, if you know what I mean.'

'I do,' I said, and she stared at me for a moment.

'In the end he changed his mind,' she went on, 'something about duty to the children.'

'In other words, someone else.'

'Of course,' she said, 'that gallumphing Annabel creature. *Such* a relief!' We both laughed again.

'But you're being a bit obvious,' she added.

'Me?'

'That lissom creature over there. The one with the big eyes.'

'Do you mean,' I asked, 'the lovely, delightful, perfect-in-every-way Mrs Barclay?'

'You'd better watch her husband. He looks vicious to me.'

'It doesn't concern me. I'm hoping to get married again soon.'

'My poor Freddie,' she said, laying her hand lightly on my arm. 'You've been hoping to get married again for six years to my certain knowledge . . . You must have given up on that one by now.' I was touched by the warmth of her pressure.

'Who knows?' I said.

'Everyone but you, it seems,' was her reply. Being an optimist, I paid no attention, but I *was* grateful when another signal announced the move back to the Library, with its blazing fire and rattling trolley complete with various flavours of oblivion.

May 1

I woke to hear the church bells ringing close by. My head! It's madness. Years ago I had a car crash. Among its good results was spectacular weight loss. On the down-side, a long operation left me somewhat depressed. It's something to do with the amount of anaesthetic. Anyway, I gave up alcohol (who needs extra depressants?), which immediately made everyone assume I had been a raging alcoholic. For four glorious years I felt like a million dollars. The silly thing is that, as many people find, alcohol doesn't agree with me, and I don't much like the taste. But it does dull the dreariness of solitude. Temporarily.

I sat up. That's IT! Not another drop till this season's over. No one should allow themselves to feel like this. George Bernard Shaw eschewed alcohol to avoid being second-rate. I shall be quite content to be able to wake up feeling fresh. But I need a good reason. The last one turned sour. Hence this headache.

When I reached the dining-room, the only inhabitant was Tony. He ignored me. I lifted the lid of the first of a series of gleaming silver dishes, and decided on a cup of tea instead. I sat down beside him. He rattled his newspaper, then looked at his watch. I could see it was a bit of a wrench. If he was going to leave, it meant abandoning those shiny sausages, that glowing yellow egg, that glistening kidney. Poor Tony, poor pinching household martinet. It was too much for him; he continued to eat. It was difficult to think of anything to say.

'I liked your slippers,' I tried. The previous evening he had been wearing a cherry-coloured smoking jacket with big woven toggles and a matching pair of velvet slippers, embroidered with some strange device – the crest, presumably, that medieval Barclays had sported while bullying their villeins; or not, as the case may be. He offered no reply.

'Was that a vole?' I persevered.

'A wyvern, actually,' he said.

'Gosh.'

I sipped my tea, listening to him chewing on the kidney.

'Here you all are!' Anthea breezed in, still in her dressing gown. 'What fun! Anything interesting in the papers?' We both rose for our morning pecks.

'I'll ring for some more coffee. Did I see Anne going off to church with George?' This was news.

'Oh, that George,' I said. 'He's incorrigible!' Tony put down his fork and left the room. It is because I see something of myself, refracted through Tony, that I am so unsympathetic, I think.

We played bridge all morning, and at lunch I was between my

hostess and Anne. Looking down the crowded table, bright with flowers and silver, I reflected on the encouraging renaissance of English country houses.

The French were lured away from theirs by Louis XIV's policy of weakening the landowners by concentrating their attention on the dotty rituals of Versailles. Château life never really recovered, although Paris has now assumed the role of Versailles as the hub of French life. Châteaux look good in the Bottin Mondain listings, but are rarely used except for hunting and the summer holidays. Central Europe has never recovered from the wars, Madrid and Lisbon echo Paris, and in America, whose great country houses are largely unknown, family pride in land has never established itself over fiscal advantage. The Irish, once the possessors of a widespread and valuable heritage in this field, have deliberately encouraged their decay in the inaccurate belief that they were the produce solely of the Anglo-Irish Ascendancy.

Only in Britain have these buildings, for 900 years the true seats and symbols of temporal power, and latterly the best examples of our national artistry, been consistently valued above short-term gain. We have lost the London palaces, but are still actually adding to the country list. The New House in Sussex and Kings Walden Bury in Hertfordshire are at least the equal of anything lost in the last twenty years. When Clive Aslet produced a fine book on Edwardian houses entitled *The Last Country Houses*, John Martin Robinson trumped it with a volume triumphantly entitled *The Latest Country Houses*! And Francis Johnson is still at it today, giving as much pleasure to other clients as he did to me when building the Pavilion, including preparing plans for a country house in Australia for the Jagelmans.

Okay, so the power has gone. In this house Bill lives, not on his farm rents, but on his income as a merchant banker. The energy of the owners, like their eighteenth-century predecessors, is expended on profitable employment. The Augustan hiccup of Victorian idleness – that respectability entailed seeking nothing beyond unearned income – has been cured by the medicine of socialism. *That* bottle can now be put at the back of the cabinet, along with leeches and syrup of figs.

May 9

A weekend in Norfolk, with Alexander out from school. We went to look at Blickling, surely the most glamorous of the Jacobean mansions, with its gay Dutch gables and pretty ogee domes. Whenever we used to perform here, we were always put firmly in the Long Gallery (long, of course, and thin, totally unsuitable) rather than in the Peter the Great Room (tall and square, perfect in every way). In those days I was inexperienced in persuading people to look clearly at their true priorities. The route from the second door we used in the Long Gallery to the changing room was so circuitous that we kept a special ball of purple wool (in fact three balls joined) known as the Blickling Ball. This was strung up stairs, down corridors, round corners so that the singers could, like Theseus, find their way through the labyrinth.

There are two aggressive questions that I frequently have to parry. One is 'Does this, er, opera thing wash its face?' (which, being translated, means 'Is it conceivable that you earn *anything* at all?') I rarely reply with other than a brassy smile. There seems no point in swapping insults with a man who sweats his way to an office every day in order to grumble about the money market, only to find himself redundant at 50.

The other is, 'What will you do when all this comes to an end?' What indeed?

Not that I can be too solemn about our life. There *is* something inherently comic about grown people gipsying around the world, putting on funny clothes and singing foreign songs to make a living.

The first year, at Thorpe Tilney, I hired a harpsichord, ten feet long, for the performance. We had been rehearsing with the piano, so on the morning of the dress rehearsal Albert, my farm foreman, and I had to swap them over. He was driving the fork-lift over the lawn with me on the lift, steadying the harpsichord, when a farm salesman came round the corner of the house. It really wasn't the time to talk about our fertilizer needs. 'Come back another time,' I suggested. That was the night of the ill-fated orchestral rehearsal. The orchestra's demise meant we had to reverse the process. So the next morning, although we were in the middle of the harvest, Albert got out the fork-lift again. He was very carefully driving me back across the lawn, hanging on to the harpsichord as before, when the same salesman strode round the corner. He stopped and stared at us for a bit.

'Still at it, then,' he said.

May 14

This is the third night running that my mother has attended. No one could have a more supportive parent. It was thanks to her that I first went to so many operas as a student. She has consistently encouraged me throughout the leaner years, employs us to put on a play every Christmas at her home, and is by far our most regular member of the audience.

Just seeing her smiling face nearby (she likes to sit near the piano to watch Bryan play) is a tonic not only to me but also to

I told you you could reach top C if I tried.

all the members of the company, who get to know her well.

Tonight Helen is singing like an angel – clear, soaring notes, of unbelievable sweetness. Her voice caresses the music – it's really impossible to describe and no doubt anything one could say would sound like something out of Pseuds Corner, particularly anything *I* say, who can't even read music. As a page-turner, I leave much to be desired. But I do know that her voice is by far the most moving of them all, and provokes the greatest emotional response, especially at such close quarters.

This is a Sotheby's evening. Grey Gowrie, their Chairman, made a good punchy speech and we all had dinner together afterwards. I had his wife, Neiti, our honorary German coach, on one side and my mother on the other, so I had a lovely evening. I don't suppose many people complain about their sponsors, but I reckon we are unusually lucky. Grey and his team are unfailingly supportive; indeed, he has rarely refused any requests I have made, even to the extent of giving Harry two days' experience in his office last month. Pavilion Opera is a natural partner for the art market, because most of the houses we visit are themselves museums of art, sometimes static, sometimes in flux, while most of our audience are buyers or sellers.

It's lovely watching Peter and Amy together. Theirs seems a completely generous love – unadulterated by the tension or jealousy that characterize one or two of our other couples. The Saturday night performance is usually the tricky one – after a week on the road, one or other is returning to another base, to other duties. Peter and Amy seem to float above this, their expressions tonight, as on other nights, cloudless and loving.

'A pretty picture, eh?' Otto, a chorus understudy, had joined me. There was a malicious glint in his expression.

'Yes,' I said. 'It is nice to see people happy.'

'We don't see that gloomy husband so often these days,' murmured Otto. 'I wonder if he's happy too.'

'Hm.' I walked off.

May 16

The way we perform is unusually accessible to children. We've done quite a few schools: Heath Mount, Stowe, Maidwell, Oakham, Cranborne Chase, Windlesham House, Haileybury (originally the training college of the East India Company, built by William Wilkins of National Gallery fame, and subsequently inflated with Sir Herbert Baker's customary bombast). Because the action is immediately in front of them and clearly comprehensible they don't seem to be alienated, as they can be by distant figures gesticulating on a stage. My regret is that, in order to provide clients with a reliability which comes expensive, we have effectively priced ourselves out of the schools' market except where, as at Stowe, a local benefactor makes it possible for them by underwriting the cost.

An exception is today, when we are doing two performances of *Don Pasquale* for Digital: one for their corporate entertainment programme, the other a matinée for school children bussed in from Birmingham.

As always, they were a lovely audience – totally relaxed and, when they find themselves laughing perhaps in spite of themselves, very enthusiastic.

We're at Ragley – Captain Hooke's major achievement as architect after the Civil War (he trained in the Engineers) to which Gibbs added, a hundred years later, his world-famous Hall, a riot of rococo plasterwork, now in pink and white as seen in the television adaptation of *War and Peace*. I think it looked more comfortable with Natasha dancing and General Kutuzov stumping about with the Czar than with seedy old Don Pasquale brushing the dust off his torn clothes. When I first looked (our first year on tour), the Red Drawing-room seemed the ideal room.

'No, thank you,' said Lord Hertford. 'The last time I moved all that furniture, I put my back out.' At that time I was afraid the Hall would be too big for us. But here we are today – no problems, and the acoustics are perfect. The park is one of the few (Windsor, Hatfield, Parham, Packington, Ickworth) which has an authentic medieval 'chase' atmosphere, wild and romantic and studded with ancient trees: not to be confused with the Arcadian perfection of the landscape architects (William Kent at Euston, for example, or 'Capability' Brown at Petworth and Sledmere, or Humphrey Repton at Attingham or Burley on-the-Hill). It has, in Bobby Corbett's favourite phrase, 'the true rust of the Barons' Wars'.

May 18

My father's memorial service this morning went off well. Helen sang 'I know that my Redeemer liveth', by which he would have been greatly moved.

Whatever the uncertainties of his life, and they were many because he was a modest man, uneasy in a crowd, who nevertheless drove himself to undergo many public commitments, he was always sustained by one inner strength: a quiet but unassailable trust in the Christian faith.

May 19

Figaro at Syon. I know I shouldn't doze at the piano. But very, very occasionally, like tonight, the eyelids begin to close, the busy world seems delightfully hushed and the next thing I know Bryan has stuck his elbow in my ribs. As a matter of fact, *he* nodded off at Sturminster Newton last year. He was still playing, but the face was definitely drooping. Noel rushed over and started shouting his recitative in Bryan's ear. I nudged him cautiously and received a gentle smile. In the interval I said nothing, but just as the lights went down for Act 2, he leant over and whispered 'Yes, I was asleep.'

May 21

Great Chalfield. Staying in this lovely wainscoted room again. It's extraordinary to think that the house was derelict when Robert Floyd's grandfather stepped in to save it in the Twenties.

After tea, Susan suggested cricket. Bruce Carter had just brought some stumps and a bat in from the big van, so we set up in the garden. The boundary was the church wall on one side, and the terrace above the canal on the other. It was great fun. Bruce hit two sixes before being caught by Noel. I hadn't played since school. When it was my turn to bat, I decided to try to get a ball right over the church. Noel bowled short and I smacked the ball as hard as I could. It flew straight at Susan's head. There was a shout and she dropped to the ground, as it whistled past her and into the yew. She laughed; I was the one in shock. I must have been *mad*. I'd nearly killed my prima donna half an hour before a performance, with her understudy two hours the other side of London.

'No more cricket until we get a tennis ball.'

Long faces (after all, it was entirely my fault for being so silly), but . . .

May 24

'What is truth?' – the question upon which rests Pontius Pilate's fragile reputation as a humourist. And yet, had he stayed for an answer, he might be there still. It must be your experience, as it is mine, that the same set of circumstances can bear a number of interpretations, all of them seemingly opposed, and yet paradoxically all also true. If this is especially valid in affairs of the heart, so too is it valid in opera. Artists can sing badly yet have their greatest effect on the audiences' heart-strings; rooms can be dingy and inappropriate, yet oddly moving. I am often astounded by people of apparent musical common sense complimenting me on the one indisputable dud of the evening; at least, Bryan and I have thought she was a dud. But if someone loved her, then she was, by definition, lovable.

Sometimes I fantasize about choosing all the worst people we audition and putting them on in a show to see what people would say. To say that there is no need because many of them are regularly available with our grander competitors would be an exaggeration. However, last year I did, unusually, terminate two contracts (paid in full, Equity please note) because I thought the people involved were so awful that I could not face presenting them, even as understudies. Today I see that both have named parts in major shows coming up. It is thus with everything: pictures, music, men and women. What nauseates one, drives another wild with passion. And yet the person, or the object, remains intrinsically the same.

May 25

It was nice to see Jane Holinshed, my sister's old friend, in the audience again tonight. George brought her and then left, saying he had a headache. We exchanged glances at this. Nothing needed to be said. She sat in the third row, at an angle from us, and yet I was able to watch her reactions throughout. Music does something very dramatic to her – at once relaxing and animating her face, so that it glows with exhilaration and the signs of strain are washed away. Glancing round the audience I noticed several of her former admirers. Ginger Alec-Smith was in the front row with his wife and parents-in-law, and there were others. Seven, in fact.

When she came to kiss me goodbye, I murmured in her ear: 'Rather a nostalgic evening for you, I thought. Quite a few old flames.'

The blue eyes went very sharp and she slapped my cheek, hard enough to sting, not hard enough to attract attention. Then she laughed. 'Yes. You're too sharp. That's your problem.'

'Eight in all,' I said, as a tease. At least this would smoke out the existence of a new lover, if there was one. And place him in this audience.

'Ye-es,' she said slowly. 'Yes.' I felt a twinge of jealousy. She pursed her lips, and then opened her mouth to let out a great gust of uninhibited laughter. Really, she is superb.

May 26

I was still asleep when the telephone rang this morning.

'SEVEN, there were only SEVEN!'

It was Jane, in a rage. I could hear George mumbling in the background. 'Use your own bathroom,' she shouted.

'Eh?'

'Not you, you fool. I'm talking to George. God knows what he caught last night.'

'I made it eight,' I said firmly, feeling absurdly pleased.

'No, you didn't,' she said. 'You were just trying to test me.' And she rang off.

May 30

Good news, and bad. Blenheim have abandoned the idea of the subservient orchestra, which may enter *after* the Duke, even though there will now be a Guest of Honour. But the big room at North Mymms has been declared unsafe. So it's back to the long, low room. Christine has been talking to the charity organizer, a nice woman who has promised to help me on the night. God knows what it will sound like. Anyway, I've dictated a letter to her explaining the problem and saying that the responsibility must, in this case, be theirs.

June 1

I was staying with my mother when Bruce Carter rang. Our Barbarina had reported sick for tonight. I got my diary, looked up Amy's number and dialled it.

'Montagu residence.' It was her husband's voice.

'Is that you, Raoul? It's Freddie.'

'Who?'

'Freddie Stockdale.' Silence. 'Pavilion Opera?' Still nothing. 'May I speak to Amy?' This time I got a sharp response.

'She's with you. She's always with you.'

Well, of course she *wasn't*. She hadn't sung with the company for nearly a fortnight.

'Oh, yes,' I said. 'It's just that I've been away. Of course she is. I'll talk to her when I get there. Thank you so much.' He hung up.

'What was that about, darling?' asked my mother, looking at me over the top of her book.

'I nearly put my foot in it,' I said. 'One of our girls has been playing truant and pretending she was with the company.'

'And that was her husband?'

'Yes. I'm afraid so. But I don't think he would have suspected too much.'

'What strange things you have to do,' she remarked, turning back to her book.

'At least, I *think* I kept my voice neutral,' I said.

'I'm sure you did, darling,' my mother said. 'You sounded tremendously neutral to me.'

June 3

Figaro at Melbourne House in Chiswick, the tall Queen Anne house which my late sister and her husband Marcus Edwards bought when they married. He has remarried and Sandra, his second wife, produces huge bowls of salmon kedgeree, followed by strawberries, to sustain us.

As this is our only annual outdoor performance – at the end of the garden, confined within a thick yew hedge – I thought I might take advantage of the Count's explicit call for fireworks to surprise the audience by letting some off during the closing bars of the opera. I had rung Christine earlier with my order: 'Not the usual little ones – I want some seriously big bangs.' They were delivered direct to Marcus this morning, and look splendidly businesslike.

While the singers rehearsed, Marcus and I dug one in behind the hedge just to amuse ourselves, as there were more than enough for the evening.

'Shall I light it?' I asked.

'Yes – go on.' I lit the fuse and stood back.

The explosion shattered the windows in the studio and was followed by an eerie silence. Not a sound. It was as if London had come to a complete halt.

'What?' I could see Marcus was mouthing something at me. Then I realized. My ears were buzzing. I had been temporarily deafened.

'I said, YOU'LL GIVE THE AUDIENCE A HEART ATTACK,' he bellowed.

Bryan came round the hedge. 'I don't think that's a good idea musically,' he said firmly. The singers came crowding round behind him, no doubt expecting to find an incinerated impresario.

'What *are* you doing?' asked Amy.

'Fireworks. We were just trying out the fireworks for the last chorus tonight.'

And that was the end of that idea. But as the last chorus approached, I watched the back row of the audience and amused myself by imagining that a dozen of those mortars were about to go off ten feet behind them. It would certainly have been a surprise . . .

June 4

Our annual visit to Jersey, to raise money for the Zoo, is a great highlight. When I was a new boy at school our employer Marcus Binney, quiet, unassuming, but supremely resolute, was a very welcome contemporary. Since then he has, almost single-handedly, promoted the cause of architectural preservation from being a patrician backwater to what it is now: a recognized national priority. He and his wife, Anne, take a personal hand in entertaining the cast, which has led to the phrase 'being Binneyed'. When we stagger down to breakfast, Marcus cooks us all eggs and bacon; when we stagger off to bed, bulging with Anne's pasta and profiteroles, they nip off to do the washing up. And wine flows like there's no tomorrow.

Tonight it's *Don Giovanni*.

Alice looked a bit uncomfortable in her first aria and shot off stage.

'Colin!!' she was scarlet with rage. 'Look at this god–damned underskirt,' she shrieked. 'It keeps twisting round my legs. *Do* something, for Chris'sake!'

'But Alice,' he said, looking at the confusion round her legs, 'You're still wearing your own skirt as well.'

Long, long pause while everyone looked away.

Then her expression changed.

'Col-lin, honey,' she cooed, 'I really do need someone to look after me, don't I?'

June 5

I've got Valentine with me (it's half-term) so today Marcus Binney took us both with his sons to visit the Germans' underground hospital. Miles and miles of creepy tunnels, excavated by slave labour imported from other countries victimized by the Third Reich. It's been converted by private enterprise into a highly profitable museum. Today it was packed. Fifty years ago – ancient history for Valentine, but uncomfortably close for me. He bought some bullets to take back to school.

June 6

Our third show here – *Figaro*.

I flew over to Guernsey in the morning in a tiny plane that climbed, as it seemed, vertically, to make the hop. If we can get contracts on both islands next year, I think I will send the cast by ferry.

A delicious lunch of local fish followed by a quick tour of a concert hall, a church and Sausmarez Manor, an oddly disappointing house with one grand façade but a jumble at the back and no big room. The Concert Hall would be best.

Roberto and Alice's scene in Act 2 was electrifying. They positively spat at each other, but when he threw over the table, an earnest little man in the audience got up from his seat, hurried over and picked it up, carefully replacing the bits and pieces on top. I could have strangled him, but the others were perfect. Alice stared at him imperiously and tilted her chin. Roberto just snapped 'Grazie', before carrying on with his recitative as if this happened every night.

June 7

Back to London. A terrible moment at Jersey airport: a deafening buzzer sounded when Valentine went through the security cage. And the bullets were confiscated! He looked as if he had lost his dearest friend. Then the Customs Officer dug in his own pocket for a note. 'I'm so sorry,' he said, giving it to Valentine. 'But buy something else in London.'

More vegetarian trauma on the plane. Phyllida had ordered six vegetarian meals, but the stewardess said she only had four. I said I was perfectly happy with an ordinary tray. Then a row started further down.

'I told you!' shouted Stefan. 'I'm never vegetarian in the air. In the *air*.'

'How can I remember that?' wailed Phyllida.

'And that girl', said the outraged stewardess, pointing down the aisle, 'says she'll make up her mind when she's seen the alternative.'

'Not on the ground!' Stefan was still calling out angrily. 'I'm *vegetarian* on the ground – except abroad.'

Phyllida put in her ear-plugs.

June 8

Figaro at Ludlow, staying with David and Marion Crawford-Clarke, an annual haven of peace and hospitality. Great excitement today. Emma has had a love letter from a member of the audience. I had already heard about it from Bruce and Bryan before she brought it to me.

> Dear Emma, if I may,
>
>   As soon as I saw you, I knew we were made for each other. You are so beautiful, so funny, so passionate, and your voice pierces my heart.
>
>   I know you are on the move, but luckily I have houses in Yorkshire, London and Dorset. If you will name a day, I will meet you at any of them so that we can get to know each other better.
>
> Yours, Goole
>
>   PS. Or I can come to you. Any day you choose.

I gave it back to her, smiling. 'You've made quite an impression.'

She grinned. 'Mmm,' she said. 'But "Goole"? That's a funny name.'

'It's a rather old-fashioned way of telling you he's Lord Goole.'

'Oh, really?' she said. 'How old is he?'

'I've no idea,' I said. 'But I can look him up.'

'What shall I do?'

'Well,' I said, thinking. 'If you don't reply he'll persist. I'm assuming you don't want to encourage him?'

'Oh, no,' she said, glancing involuntarily at Ron who was making two cups of coffee in a corner. 'Oh, no.'

'Well,' I said, 'I'll draft a letter tomorrow and you copy it out and sign it. That will deal with it.'

'No earls write to me,' grumbled Otto, the bass baritone, tossing his head as she walked away. 'I'd give them something to write about, I can tell you.'

June 9

Researches in Debrett reveal that the lovesick Earl of Goole is unmarried, and 36. The reference book is less expansive than he on his territorial possessions – chronicling Yorkshire and London, but drawing a veil of secrecy over Dorset.

Lord Goole

Dear Lord Goole, [I wrote, resisting the original temptation of 'Dear Goole']

Thank you for your kind letter. Naturally I was flattered that my acting made such an impression on you. But it was only acting, and I have to tell you that I am very happily married and we are expecting our first child at Christmas.

I do hope I have not caused you unhappiness through portraying my role in the opera.

Yours etc. Emma

'But I'm not!' protested Emma when I showed it to her.
'Not what?'
'Not pregnant. That's a direct lie.'
'I know,' I said patiently, 'but it's the clinching factor. Men will clamber over almost any obstacle to pursue a woman if they think they have the smallest gleam of hope. But expecting another man's child is usually seen as demanding withdrawal, even if only temporarily.'
'Oh?' She pursed her lips. 'Well, thank you, Freddie. You've been a great help.' And she seized the letter and went off to her room to copy it.

June 10

My job is often to act as mediator between cast, audience and employer. Often they will have different, irreconcilable needs. How best to square the circle?

Tonight we're rehearsing with the orchestra in Ely Cathedral. It's bitterly cold inside; eight centuries of fen winters have left their mark. The strings say their fingers won't respond. What can I do?

I find the splendidly cheerful verger. He gets the Precentor. At last the Dean arrives.

'What can I do to help?' he asks courteously.
'We've got to raise the temperature,' I explain. 'The violinists just can't play.'

He names a grand London orchestra who had no problems a

month ago. We work our way through the point that what matters is tomorrow's performance, not those in the past.

'Well,' he said, 'I will turn on the heating if you like.'

My spirits rose; another problem solved.

'But,' he added, 'it takes three days to raise the ambient temperature by one degree.' Impasse. I've seen the players. It's not an idle complaint – their fingers (and mine) are stiff and sore.

'I'll tell you what I'll do,' suggested the Dean, a man of positive action. 'I'll try to commandeer some oil stoves, and we'll put them round the orchestra; it won't make much difference, but they'll feel we're trying.'

Within an hour he was back with ten stoves, and I spent the rest of the day recovering them from various pilferers – the bookstand, the Friends' table – who understandably wanted to join in!

Not everyone was on my side. I attracted the attention of another Church dignitary, who had expected to let us some rooms at a profit: I was able to find cheaper accommodation. He stumped right across the chancel to hiss in my face, 'You won't live long, the way you go on!'

Murder in the Cathedral? Surely not. I think he meant I am too overwrought. Time for dinner.

June 11

A very moving performance. The orchestra, buttressed by the glowing stoves, played beautifully. Most of the audience were muffled up in blankets, and Alice sang like an angel.

Earlier in the day someone had come to complain that the door was jammed open (to bring in our props). I went to investigate, to be met by a comforting blast of *warm* air. After all, the sun is shining outside.

'Quick,' I said, 'where's the Dean?'

As I'd expected, he took the point, and from then on we kept the doors wide open.

We started late, and as the light began to fade the most gorgeous shadows began to creep across the walls, the side aisles retreated into mysterious voids and the whole building seemed to vibrate and hum with the music.

Every now and then I am transported by the happiness of the moment. 'If I never do another show,' I thought, 'this has made it all worth while.'

June 16

A quick visit to Paris, promised to Valentine if he learned to swim. Last month he proudly produced a certificate, and here we are.

Today we had breakfast in our room, then a very short visit to the Louvre, mainly to see the Pyramide, ices at Angelina's, three hours going up the dreaded Eiffel Tower, and a very late lunch. He ordered Tournedos Rossini, then asked for tomato ketchup. I thought we'd be thrown out. Instead, in the conventionally grand Parisian restaurant, the waiter positively beamed, and fetched the familiar red bottle.

Turning down a little side street in the afternoon, we found ourselves in a civic building with an anteroom consecrated to the dead of two World Wars. Unlike the English memorials, the lists here were of equal length – the latter with the names of many women. What tragedy, for example, befell Jeanne and Marcel Guillan? These men and women, the inscription read, were those: *'fusillés, massacrés, exterminés par la barbarie et la trahison qui se sont sacrifiés pour que:*

VIVE LA FRANCE'

I explained all this to Valentine, who is only eight, and we walked for a while in silence.

We played scrabble all evening, and he had his first snail at dinner with friends. We have just got in at one in the morning,

after wandering round the streets, admiring the Place Vendôme
and stopping off at a couple of bistros for hot chocolate. We are
both playing truant – a happy day.

June 19

Oh dear, oh dear. Tonight was rather awful. We were doing
Elisir d'amore, a deliciously light-hearted and funny opera by
Donizetti, with some heart-rending love duets. I have always
directed the love scenes seriously (as opposed to the usual clichéd
burlesque) because I cannot accept that someone who sings of
hopeless passion as tenderly as Nemorino does, can be a pathetic
buffoon. Anyway, there we were, or rather there they were,
two lovers getting on each other's nerves, when I noticed a
rather extraordinary sight opposite. A man and a woman were
sitting side by side at the end of a row. He was getting paler, she
was turning pink, then scarlet. It was like one of those chemistry
tests, getting the liquid out of one test-tube into another. I
couldn't stop watching. Just as his face seemed almost to
disappear, so hers grew positively purple. Suddenly, as I
watched, he slowly keeled over with a terrific crash, taking his
chair with him. The woman didn't move a muscle – she had
obviously guessed what was going to happen. Perhaps he did
this often? Nemorino cast a single ghastly look at me, and I
glared back. The show must go on. Several people in the
audience were picking the invalid up. Bryan played on grimly,
and I saw Bruce appear in the doorway with some of the house
staff. Three men were trying to carry the body across the third
row. While everyone else made way, a young buffer stayed
firmly put, one tweeded, uncompromising knee across the
other, his face blue and disapproving. As the cortège passed in
front of him, he craned over it so as not to miss the opera's
rather half-hearted action. I heard later that a doctor had revived
the patient, but that his condition was very serious.

June 20

Don Pasquale at Goodwood. The ubiquitous James Wyatt
started building a colossal flint octagon for the then Duke of
Richmond at the end of the eighteenth century. Only the first
three sides were completed, an omission for which the
descendants may well be grateful. It is still a sizeable house,
crouching in its magnificently wooded park.

Alice was wonderful tonight – I don't think I've mentioned
how very funny she can be. Her wit comes out in her expression
and her way of delivery, rather than in the precise words. And it
is made all the sharper by glinting through her imperturbable
good nature.

June 23

It's getting worse. Coming along the corridor to bed just now, I
heard extraordinary noises coming from one of the rooms.
Now, normally this would signal 'keep well away'. But these
were gargling, hiccuping shrieks.

I knocked – no change. Gingerly, I opened the door. There
was Ron, rolling on the bed, apparently in a fit, while Noel and
Helen knelt praying beside him.

Helen saw me and put her finger to her lips. She tiptoed
outside. 'Ron's *very worried* about his performance.'

So am I.

" What do you mean –
I sang the first verse well?"

June 25

Yesterday was *Figaro* at Lancaster House. A boiling hot day. As soon as I got there I drew the curtains to try to mitigate the effect. There is an air-conditioning system but, as usual, it is almost imperceptible. Still, by seven o'clock the temperature is bearable.

A first quick check on the cast, and particularly Enid's costume, and then I went to sit down by the piano. It was like going into an oven. What had happened? Some idiot had opened the windows, letting in the stifling air from the street. I rushed over and closed them again, exciting angry protests from a particularly obstreperous old man at the back. I tried to explain, but he wouldn't listen. It was no surprise to learn that he was a celebrated philosopher.

Finally I got everything in reasonable order and the performance started. From time to time I could hear rumblings of discontent from the centre of the opposition. It was, indeed, unbearably hot, but this could only be rectified if we kept the windows *closed*. Try explaining that to a Fellow of All Souls who is perfectly convinced that he knows best.

Anyway, on we went, and the end of the last act approached. The key is that the Count (sung tonight by George Mosley) has, as he thinks, caught the Countess in an adulterous embrace with Figaro. He seizes the cloaked and hooded figure, gathers the others around, and prepares to denounce her. At this moment the real Countess (for it is Susanna under the hood) comes up behind him, and the humiliation is his instead. A marvellous moment. George grabbed the disguised Helen, flung her down; the others knelt. Bryan played Alice's entrance.

Nothing.

A terrible, terrible pause.

He played a variation on it, slightly louder.

Nothing.

Everything froze. It seemed like half an hour. Then George turned and walked out of the room.

Off home? How long would the others stay there before losing their nerve?

Suddenly the door flew open and George returned, dragging a very pale Alice.

She sang her piece and the opera ended in undeserved applause. Naturally I was boiling – I worked my way quickly through the crowd. Too late; as I neared the staircase I saw two figures scuttling out – Alice and another girl.

'What happened, Alice?' I asked her the next day.

'We-ell, Fred-dee', she said slowly, 'you see-ee . . .'

'No,' I said. 'Tell me, please.'

'Well, I was just listening to her love life, and it was so-oo-oo sad.'

Sad! I was really angry, and Alice wouldn't speak to me afterwards. But she, indeed all of us, were lucky that George had such presence of mind. But I always forgive her, because she has such a beautiful voice and such charisma on stage.

June 26

A parcel of letters arrived from Thorpe Tilney and Bruce Carter started handing them out.

'Any for me?' asked Emma.

'You're not expecting one from Lord Goole?' I asked, I don't quite know why.

'No,' she said, but without an answering smile.

'When did you post that letter?'

'Seventeen days ago,' she said, without a pause. So precise? Was she counting?

June 28

The great bonus of producing the book of opera synopses, delivered today, is that it has made me do some research. Nothing have I enjoyed more than reading Ernest Newman's four-volume *Life of Wagner*. A wholly unappreciated wedding present, it has sat ignored in the library for more than twenty years; now I can hardly put it down. Two quotes give an admirable and accurate description of the frustrations of promoting live performances:

> But before a note of the overture [of Wagner's *Das Liebesverbot*] was sounded, bedlam broke loose behind the scenes. The husband of the leading lady, the charming Frau Pollert, made for her lover (the second tenor) and smote him on the nose, concentrating a whole season's marital rancour in the blow. Frau Pollert tried to appease her husband, received a castigation that was no doubt well deserved, and went off with hysterics. The rest of the company took sides according to their sympathies, the occasion being warmly welcomed as a heaven-sent one for working off all the professional animosities and jealousies that had been accumulating. There was nothing for it but for the manager to appear before the curtain and inform the infinitesimal audience that owing to unforeseen circumstances there would be no performance that evening.

The early days of Pavilion Opera to the life! And again:

> At Dresden, the first oboe indulged at the rehearsal of Berlioz's concert in frills and mordents in his solo at the commencement of the *scène aux champs* in the *Symphonie Fantastique*. Berlioz pointed out to him the error of his ways; but at the concert, the oboist, knowing that the composer could not interfere with him then, indulged to his heart's content in his favourite pastime of embroidering the melody in the Italian fashion, regarding the maddened Berlioz all the time with a cunning air.

That rings a few bells, too.

July 4

We do get rather spoiled in the west country. Tonight it's *Don Giovanni* at Yarlington, a delicious red-brick manor house stuffed with more Napoleonic relics than Malmaison, and glamorous blonde daughters round every corner. This is our sixth or seventh year; lots of laughter, home-made ice-cream and some panic about the space. Charles and Carolyn de Salis always provide a cheerful, alert audience which makes a big contribution to the evening. The A303 is an unpredictable road – tonight two of the cast were an hour late, so I had begun to worry about summoning reserves when suddenly they hurried in, angry with themselves for missing tea.

We always try to put in some reference to Napoleon because of the very marked focus of the house's contents. The best was in *Elisir d'amore* when, unknown to me, Noel had specially drilled the soldiers who come in at the end (where they have a single line with a catchy musical phrase): their hats were all sideways, their right arms tucked into their tunics, and their message that night, delivered with great gusto, was 'non sta sera, Josephina'.

I'm afraid *Don Giovanni* provides no such opening, but there were more demands for Roberto tonight. One woman, eyes glittering, asked me for his telephone number. I darted backstage to ask Bryan's advice. It was characteristically straightforward: 'Why not?' I don't know why I asked.

July 5

Our annual visit to Elton, very popular with the cast who are cosseted by Merrie Proby's luxurious hospitality, especially the chocolate mousse.

'Can I talk to you sometime?'

It was Amy. Her dark eyes were troubled within the heavy make-up of a *Rigoletto* courtesan.

'In the interval?'

'No, somewhere quiet.'

'Okay,' I said, 'let's meet in that little room there after the show. Join me there when you've let Colin have your costume.'

Immediately after the performance I went and waited for her. It was a warm night so I opened the window and sat leafing through the schedule.

'I'm so sorry to bother you,' she said, coming in and shutting the door.

'Don't be silly. It's what I'm here for.'

She sat down and there was a long silence which I did not break. Eventually she looked up. 'You know about Peter and me.'

There wasn't much point in prevaricating. I smiled. 'Yes.'

'Are you very shocked?'

'Of course not. We don't sit in judgement on each other.'

'Raoul said he spoke to you.'

'Yes,' I said. 'I don't think I said anything to disturb him unduly.'

'Thank you,' she said; then, 'Weren't you very embarrassed?'

'It wasn't the first time it's happened.'

'With Raoul?' She looked genuinely frightened.

'No, no – with others.'

'Oh.' Was she disappointed? Was passion restricted to just Peter and herself?

'I'm going to tell him.'

'Do you think that's wise?'

'That's what I wanted to ask you. I talked to Bryan, and he said you would give me good advice.' Oh, thanks, I thought.

'It seems so mean to deceive Raoul. I hate lying.'

'Sometimes its kinder to keep one's burdens to oneself.'

'But shouldn't he have the chance to have his say?'

I thought about this. It's one of the great dilemmas of marriage. Is the trust between partners a greater abstract

162

imperative than sparing the other unnecessary, even deliberate, pain? To confess a betrayal which is a continuing betrayal only adds to the pain. To confess a past betrayal surely produces pain for no better reason than to lighten one's own conscience. Is not the only possible reason to release the other to seek solace of their own which they might otherwise feel bound to refuse?

'Do you think he would then feel free to look around for himself?' I asked gently.

'Oh, no,' she said. 'He adores me. He'd *never* have an affair with anyone else!'

'So what's the point?'

'Because I can't bear the deceit.' She burst into tears.

I opened the door. Two of the singers were standing outside, and immediately walked back into the dressing room opposite. I shut it again and came back to her.

'My advice is, don't tell him. If you do, the most likely thing is that he will try to persuade you to give Peter up. Could you do that?'

She wiped her nose and stared up at me in amazement. 'Of course not. It's quite different with Peter. He's so kind.'

'Yes, yes,' I said, anxious not to be drawn too deeply into her confidence. 'But that underlines my point. You will lose his trust anyway, and you will have destroyed his peace of mind.'

'But he keeps asking,' she cried. 'I can't bear going home. I can't bear it any more.'

I sat for a long time with her until the sobbing died down. There was a tap on the door.

'What is it?' I snapped.

'It's me,' said Colin's voice. 'We're just leaving.'

I took her out to her car. Peter was sitting in it. He did not look at me. I went across to my own car, and drove back to London, trying to deaden my feelings with a Beethoven tape.

July 6

I spent most of this morning with my solicitors. Three years reading Law taught me one thing – don't complain about judgments being unfair. The law enforces what is written, not what ought to have been written. I draw up and sign about three hundred contracts a year, congratulating myself on what my education is saving me. Then I make a mistake like this one, a muddle over understudy fees, and I am covered in confusion.

'Only someone who has studied law,' smiled my solicitor, 'could possibly have got themselves into such a tangle.' It's going to be expensive. As I left the office, I heard her murmur to her secretary, 'A little knowledge is a dangerous thing!'

July 7

Figaro at Moor Place in Hertfordshire. It's rather a surprising house, because the gates are in the main street. But once through them, you immediately leave the built up area and wind through a large park to a very dignified red-brick house, simple Baroque if that's not a contradiction in itself, with pretty blue shutters. Tordie Norman masterminds the spectacular flower arrangements, while Bryan Norman, her husband, supervises his obedient house party with infectious gaiety and enthusiasm.

'Do you actually like people clapping the arias?' he asked tonight.

Well, the truth is I don't, because it interrupts the drama, especially in the tragedies. But the singers love it. So I decided to support them.

'Oh, yes!' I said. 'The more the merrier!'

Well, I should have known better.

As soon as the audience assembled, he leapt up. 'Now then, you lot!' he cried. 'Freddie doesn't think you clap enough. So give it all you've got.'

Well, of course, all the audience stared at me, by the piano.

'That's that,' I thought. 'Now they'll never clap again' – turning redder than any known beetroot. But they were generous and clapped like mad, laughing all the time.

'That better?' demanded my host.

July 8

'Emma's had another letter from that Duke or whoever,' murmured Otto as I came in to take the rehearsal. After tea I found her standing in a doorway, gazing into space.

'Emma,' I said, 'I can't believe Lord Goole has written back.'

'Oh, yes,' she said, with a little smile. 'He's asked me to spend a weekend in Monte Carlo.'

'Monte Carlo?' I'm surprised it wasn't Baden Baden.

'All very respectable, Freddie,' she said firmly, looking at me severely.

'Oh, of course,' I agreed. 'But I just can't believe he'd have written back after that letter you sent.'

'Well, I did change it a little,' she said.

July 10

Well, well. The apotheosis of Roberto as Don Giovanni. Having directed the customary queue of nubile fans towards the dressing room tonight, I was drawn aside by a woman who had held back from the clamour.

'I want to paint him,' she said, once we were alone.

'Paint him?'

'His portrait.'

'Oh.'

'I will wait until he is free,' she said, looking gloomily at the line of self-conscious girls. 'You think he might agree?'

'I should think he will be most flattered,' I replied truthfully. She smiled.

Alan has bicycled here, all the way from Bewdley. He is very sunburnt, and justifiably proud of himself. It is a Herculean feat.

'I was nearly knocked into a ditch by a lorry,' he said, laughing.

'Please don't tell me,' I begged. He is irreplaceably good, both as an actor and as a stentorian bass. And, even more important, like Arthur he has that priceless gift of consideration for others, of being genuinely concerned.

July 12

Serious panic – we've picked up 'flu somewhere. Colin is out of action, Nicky and Enid can hardly speak, Helen (Susanna) and Alice (Countess) are both afflicted, though they stoutly insist they'll be fit tomorrow. The trouble is that Caroline is understudying both parts. And Helen and Alice are the two Norinas, so we cannot even do *Don Pasquale*.

The news of Roberto's proposed portrait has *not* been well received by the other men in the company.

'No one's ever painted *me*!' grumbled Otto, pushing out his lips in a discontented *moue*.

'But you're not Don Giovanni, darling,' said Emma, who was passing.

'Puh-leeze!' he groaned, hand on hip and examining his reflection in a mirror.

July 13

Figaro at the Laing Gallery, Newcastle. Bryan went to see Helen
and Alice this morning. They're both as bad as each other,
streaming, coughing. Alice said she'd have to stay in bed, so I
rang Caroline and she's on the train up. Now Helen's got a
temperature of 102°, so Alice says she'll sing if Caroline will
swap. I met the train.

'How wonderful to see you, Caroline!'

'That's all right, Freddie. I've been studying the score for the
Countess on the way up.'

'Ah,' I said. 'But there's a new problem.'

'Yes?' Caroline's eyes go bright and beady when she scents
trouble. Was I going to tell her she wouldn't be performing after
all?

'I'm afraid Helen is even worse than Alice. Could you face
singing Susanna instead of the Countess?'

She gulped. You see, the problem is that the two characters
have quite a lot of duets and dialogue together. It was madness
to make her understudy both.

'Yes, of course,' she smiled bravely. But the eyes had become
rather blurred.

Susan went on instead of Enid, and the two of them did really
well. The only problem was when Susan (as Cherubino) hid
behind one door and Caroline (Susanna) acted it as if she was
behind another. The audience can hardly have failed to be
bemused by this, but generously no one said anything. Alice was
a heroine, with Bruce and Matt, in the guise of attentive
servants, bringing her endless cups of hot lemon and honey.

July 14

Figaro at Sledmere. This time it's Alice in bed and Helen coping
bravely. Caroline, as the Countess, was totally assured.

'I suppose you'll want me as Marcellina tomorrow,' she

murmured as I congratulated her afterwards.

At least we've now got two days to recuperate at Thorpe Tilney.

July 17

Figaro at Callaly, a pretty Georgian castle with elephantiasis in its wings. One block here, one block there – but it is very handsome. I went there years ago when the Browns had it. The squire spent an enormous amount of time trying to trace his descent from its earliest, medieval owners. Finally, giving up hope, he printed a private guide-book which was circumspect about the succession. And bingo! a researcher came up with a link, so the guide-book was over-printed with a footnote establishing this claim of rather limited and personalized interest.

If Marcus Binney has done most to alert us all, from Ministers to tourists, to the need to save our architectural heritage, Kit Martin has done most in terms of physical action. Dingley, Hazells, Cullen, Gunton, Tyninghame and Callaly – a colossal accumulation of stones and bricks saved and put to practical use by his highly successful method of dividing these great

"Madam thought you needed this."

mammoths into discrete yet harmonizing residences. It is perhaps the greatest architectural success story of the last half of the century. (I suppose Lutyens takes the first half.)

Anyway, here we are, doing *Figaro* in the beautiful double-height Rococo hall with its empty niches still awaiting the Jacobite revival after two hundred and forty-five years of subtle loyalty. It's freezing cold but the caterers are well-drilled, keeping everyone tanked up with sausage rolls and champagne. The only disaster, an assistant stage manager falling downstairs and breaking an ankle, happened off-stage. She was very brave and we whisked her off to hospital without anyone noticing.

It was one of the nights when I was persuaded to ask the audience to stay in place while a magazine photographer took a quick picture of cast and onlookers. Quick? Half an hour at least. They'd better be good.

July 18

Oh, God! One of the Count's understudies was on and there was a mirror in the room. Every time he passed it, he would stop and gaze raptly at the gorgeous sight. Even when his legs carried him on in accordance with the production, his trunk would linger; last to catch up was his head, still craning backwards for a final fond look.

As for the love scenes! Poor Susanna, she said afterwards she had never felt less attractive. It's a curious thing that whereas the average Count needs little persuading to kiss his Susanna on her lips or breasts, the others WILL lay their heads confidingly on her shoulder.

'She's not your mother!' I shriek. Everybody looks at the floor. Susanna rolls her eyes and the miscreant makes a move. Then we try again. We get it right in rehearsal and then tonight, it's wrecked. What's more, I've just heard that none of the Callaly photographs have come out.

July 19

To Mellerstain, one of Robert Adam's castles, bleak granite on the outside, ravishing painted plasterwork within. *Don Giovanni* with Dr Gian Carlo Menotti in the audience. Years ago he bought Yester, one of William Adam's most beautiful houses, the childhood home of the petrifying Clemmie Waring.

'Imagine!' she said to me in great disgust. 'A Doctor! I never *did* approve of the National Health Service.' It did seem rather extraordinary, but no one knew better, to contradict her. He's asked me to lunch tomorrow – and I have eagerly accepted.

The best thing today was solving the secret of the *Lucia* dance cries. The Scots have this special sound and I have known I haven't got it right. Before tea I suddenly thought that Binning, our host, might help. I found him in front of the television.

'Can you teach them how to make that proper yelping noise?'

Oh, how I knew his expression. It said 'Please! – you can't be asking me this.' He seemed to shrink into his chair, and of course I immediately took it back. It was a fearfully intrusive idea. 'Not another thought,' I reassured him, and went back to the dining-room where the singers were tucking in to the chocolate mousse.

'I tried,' I explained. 'We still haven't got it right.'

'Eeee-up!!' A faint cry echoed from the distance.

'Eeee-up!!' It was getting nearer.

'EEEEE-UPP!!!' Binning burst through the door, his glasses sparkling and his mouth in a broad smile. First he made the men try it, then the women. Then together. Then I had to do it. After this I left, but long after the singers had dispersed to their dressing room, isolated cries could be heard along the corridors and up the stairwells.

'Eeeeeeeeeee-------uppppppppppp-P.' Well, now we know.

July 20

Lunch at Yester, served by a wizened manservant who spoke, if at all, with a Glaswegian-Italian accent. Dr Menotti has restored a lot of the house – it has wonderful plasterwork and a very grand double-height Saloon. Afterwards, the others explored the gardens while we discussed the horrors of trying to promote opera as a business rather than as a 'charity'. He says that he put on *The Medium* on Broadway, financed just like a conventional show, and it did make money – for a while. He also said that directing Pavarotti had been a great pleasure. He likes our Don, but not our Donna Elvira.

'Do they not know the word "*piano*"?' All too well, I thought. A generous and kind-hearted man.

July 21

By the time we got to Birkhill, an eighteenth-century house baronialized by Bryce, everyone was exhausted. Siobhan Dundee had organized everyone's accommodation, including some in one of the holiday cottages. We all had an uproarious dinner and went to bed early.

I was woken by a knocking on the door. 'Who is it?'
'Noel.'
'What's the time?'
'Midnight.'
That's odd, I thought, he's not staying in the house. I went to the door. His clothes were dripping.

'Look, Freddie, I'm terribly sorry to disturb you, but the others just can't cope with their rooms. There's water running down the walls and the bed linen is soaked.' This was the holiday cottage.

'Oh, God.' I didn't even know where the Dundees were sleeping. I banged on the first door. It was Bryan's. I tried a second. A child. Eventually I found them. Alexander Dundee was heroic. He pulled on some plus-fours, got out his Volvo and was off with Noel to rearrange the accommodation. We waited. And waited. Two o'clock came. Eventually, six muddy creatures floundered in. Apparently Alexander had got them all in his car, backed down the track, and got stuck. They then all got out to push him and were smothered in mud. Then his battery gave out. So they walked.

'Weren't they very cross?' I asked Noel the next morning.

'No,' he said. 'We kept agreeing: they'd never believe this at Covent Garden!'

July 22

Here we are – back at St Maur, temperamentally-speaking the most over-heated house on the Borders. The problem here is that our employer always disappears as soon as we arrive. This is an advantage in that it lowers the temperature. But it's a disadvantage if, like today, there is something wrong. This time it was the piano – placed *behind* the first row of seats.

St Maur, North Britain.

'I'm afraid you can't move the piano,' said her secretary very firmly.

'We can't perform with it there.'

'The piano has to stay', she said very deliberately, 'where it is.'

I possessed two useful bits of knowledge: first, that the bathroom of the part of the house where Mary St Maur locks herself in faces the front; second, that every year she always warns us not to damage the gateway arch with the lorry.

This year the lorry is bigger than ever. Very, very slowly Bruce reversed it towards the precious arch.

There was a screech:

'WATCH OUT! CAN'T YOU SEE THE ARCH??'

She had flung up the window and leaned out in horror.

'Mary! Hello!' I cried. 'There you are. We need your help downstairs.'

July 23

Very bad-tempered breakfast this morning. I came down past Peter, one of the tenors, who was pacing up and down the corridor. He ignored my greeting.

In the kitchen I found Susan eating Weetabix.

'Peter looks rather grim,' I said. She started laughing.

'You must ask Eddie about that.' At this point Ron came in, snatched a piece of toast, and hurried out. I stared after him.

'Am I mad, or has Ron got a black eye?' Susan started laughing again, then Eddie put his head through the hatch.

'All clear?' he asked her.

'Yes. Tell Freddie about last night.'

Well, apparently Peter and Ron had both fancied their chances with Julie, the temporary seamstress. Leaving their bedrooms, they had crept along the corridors in time-hallowed tradition, meeting face to face outside her room. A terrible whispered row had turned into a proper fight. Then they had both slunk back to bed.

'But how did you know?' I asked him.

Oh, well,' he said, assuming a modest expression, 'I got there before them.'

July 24

A cross-country route to Broughton, a very grand but very cosy late medieval castle guarding its meadows in Oxfordshire. I had a quick lunch with friends and sat and smoked by the drive. We were being interviewed by Antony Hopkins for a radio show there and I wanted to decide on what message to put across. It is always the same: opera is fun, come and enjoy it with us.

When I drove in, there were two or three people staring up at the castle chimneys. The radio team were already there. Lady Saye and Sele was finishing off some delicious shepherd's pies while fielding questions about why her husband had retired to the roof.

'He finds it very quiet up there,' she explained, while advising the interviewer not to attempt the ascent.

Outside someone thought they had spotted him, but his wife was sure he would be out of sight.

July 25

Figaro at Burley-on-the-Hill, a spreading late-Baroque house with a forecourt second only to St Peter's, where Rosalind Hanbury, most generous of hostesses, always provides the cast with a gigantic supper. More to the point, she always provides me with a bridge four for the afternoon to keep me calm. I was playing with her against two of her house party and we'd hardly dealt before there was a tremendous thud behind me. Then another. I got up and opened the door into the hall.

'For God's sake shut the door! The strings are going!'

174

The piano tuner, white-faced, was gesticulating at me. I shut the door and there was another resounding thud.

The Burley piano is not one of Bryan's favourites, hence the tuner's efforts. In vain; half way through the overture, the keys started sticking. As Bryan played, getting more and more angry, I frantically pushed the keys up with one hand while trying to turn the pages with the other. The sound was terrible. The odd thing was that when he tried it that afternoon, there had been no problem.

I tried pulling at the fillet in front of the keys. Immediately they righted themselves. I had a cheque book in my pocket, so I pulled off the cover, bent it three or four times and inserted the resulting wedge into the crack. All was well. But what a performance! When Bryan gets angry, he fairly attacks the music. We tore through the opera, sparkling, accelerating, the singers catching his mood and tossing off their recitative in spitfire form. But it also cast shadows across the drama.

'Why have you made it so bleak?' one girl asked me afterwards.

'Marriage *is* bleak,' I replied. 'It was never intended to be a farce.'

But she's right. I have cast too strong a spotlight on the sadnesses, at the expense of the comedy.

Emma was collected by a chauffeur-driven car after the show. She waved at us gaily as it drew away from the curb. Someone swore.

July 26

A minor detour to show my children the ruins of Kippax, once the longest façade in Europe. We drove up and down the lanes leading to where I remembered visiting its colossal wreck, still hugely impressive.

At last I found a lodge and then, along a cart-track, a single gate pier, heralding the demesne.

But no, there was nothing but the wide, empty fields, covering the site of that ambitious extravagance.

'*What* an interesting excursion,' said Harry. The others were silent.

July 28

Hinton St Mary, where the Pitt-Riverses have created a vast and beautiful new garden. This morning I was woken by one of the tenors trying to sing the bass aria from *Don Carlos*. Truly, people are never satisfied. Most basses long to be tenors, if only for the money and the attention. Lincolnshire Education Committee used to struggle with a similar problem, the strange tastes of the neighbouring villages of Wellingore and Navenby. The residents of Wellingore became convinced that Navenby school was better. So every morning a little crocodile of children would set off across the fen. Through summer rain and winter storms, they would trudge daily in search of an educational El Dorado. And who were these phantoms coming to meet them through the swirling snowflakes? – yes, the children of Navenby, on their way to the school in Wellingore.

July 29

I love going to Alresford in Hampshire, Admiral Rodney's house in the eighteenth century, now lived in by Virginia and Peter Constable Maxwell and all their children. They came to a local show during our first tour, and have employed us ever since.

It's a narrow room, so the *Don Giovanni* sword fight is

especially nerve-wracking. I had been prepared to cut it rather than risk endangering the audience, but Virginia got the seats well back, and it went splendidly.

'You must be their professor. You look like you've got problems.' It was a train conductor at Grand Central Station, New York, who first alerted me to one of the by-products of dragging this rollicking group of schizophrenics around the world. I now look far older than I am. I've got quite used to being asked about my younger brother Tommy (he is seven years older), but tonight was the limit.

Bryan was sitting on a sofa with an old lady after the show. I joined them, squatting on a stool.

'I used to dance with your Uncle Min,' she said. (He died, aged 80, some years ago.)

'Ah!' I said. Uncle Min was famous in his day. I particularly remember his ponderous advice, over lunch at his club, as to how best to make love in a grouse butt while keeping your head, still and apparently alert, above the heather line.

'Oh, yes,' she said. 'And do you remember General Sotheby? Wasn't he splendid! But he would be a bit older than you . . . perhaps?'

The trouble with knowing Bryan so well is that I know what

Uncle Min on the Moors.

is going to set him off. I tried not to, but I did catch just a glimpse of his eyeballs, shifting for a fatal exchange of looks. For the next five minutes I had to fight to batten down those terrible irrepressible bubbles that kept building up inside and threatened to come out in discourteous peals of laughter.

July 30

Bad news. A friend passed on a rumour: a disgruntled employer is complaining that my crew have been stealing his drink *as usual*! Nothing is impossible, but I doubted this. Yesterday I traced the source, and learned worse. 'It was exactly what they did at Callaly too!' Callaly!

So today I rang Kit Martin and asked for his version. He was horrified that I had heard, and repeated over and over again that the cast were welcome to as much drink as they wanted. He had told his story as a joke, not as a complaint. It was nice of him to emphasize this, but I still had to get to the bottom of the story.

'But what did happen?' I asked him.

It turned out that the hotel where the cast were staying had found several empty champagne bottles in one of our rooms. Prima-facie evidence indeed!

Then I rang the 'culprits'.

They were equally horrified.

'But he begged us to take them. He said we could take as many as we wanted because they were left over.'

'Who is "he"?' I asked grimly.

'The caterer, of course.'

Of course! Why not? Kit was paying. It was pure profit for the caterer, plus gratitude as well. I think they should have seen through it. But they didn't. Back to Kit, who utterly refused to be reimbursed.

New rules will be needed. From today.

July 31

Figaro at Whatton, Mike Crawshaw's grand stone house
dominating its hill outside Loughborough. He has an ingenious
carpenter called Sid who delights in providing us with special
equipment to use on the large swimming pool next to where we
perform. We had a gondola for *Hoffmann*, a drawbridge for
Lucia, and now an extended platform over the water for *Figaro*.
Every year someone nearly falls in, to give the audience a *frisson*.
This year I decided to give them what I thought they'd like – a
real immersion – breaking Alfred Hitchcock's famous rule: if
you show the audience a bomb, never let it go off. That
explodes the tension.

Antonio, our stage gardener, is a good sport. I explained the
whole thing to him. Amazingly, he agreed.

'The audience will *love* it,' I said.

He beamed. 'Anything for a laugh, eh?'

At the end of Act 2, on comes Antonio. He nearly falls in.
The quartet comes to an end, Count Almaviva orders him off,
he steps back and SPLASH! He completely disappeared. Bruce
Carter ran to the side and caught a despairing hand. The sodden
figure crawled out and ran dripping to the changing room.

Gales of applause? Not a bit of it. The audience sat in stony
silence, obviously bemused, perhaps even disapproving.

'Well done!' I said in the interval as he sat shivering in a
bathrobe, sipping hot chocolate.

'Did they love it?' he asked eagerly.

'*Adored* it! Didn't you hear the laughter?'

'No,' he said. 'I must have been under the water longer than I
thought.'

August 2

It is a source of strength and of weakness to be able to look your audience in the eyes. If they're loving it, of course this lends additional encouragement to the cast and they give even more of themselves in the building up of sympathy between the two groups. But if they're hating it?

I discovered this first at Burton Constable, a massive Jacobean hulk anchored unexpectedly in the flat marshes beyond Beverley in the East Riding. When we went there, ten years ago, the exterior had been newly repainted so that the coat of arms above the door was gleaming with yellow ochre instead of gold. This was the first of many jarring notes that evening. Our host was generous and courteous and brought me a whisky and soda in his dressing gown after a minor fracas when his wife took some of her friends into the changing room to stare at the singers getting undressed.

The land lies level in every direction and, looking out of the western windows, I noticed some splendid statues rearing out of the twilight. Letting myself out, I walked towards them, increasingly uneasy at what seemed (without my glasses) to be their rather weird silhouettes. As I got closer, I saw that there were huge gaps, gaping craters, missing limbs replaced by stumpy spikes of metal. I stared at these grotesques and then understood. They were plaster statues, cast perhaps by the British Museum workshop, but they had been put in the open. A few northern frosts and they were, of course, falling to pieces. Even marble is best swathed against East Riding winters – it was a melancholy sight.

Back to the show, with the singers still worrying about further invasion.

We started and there wasn't a ripple of interest. Climaxes came and went. Finales were ignored. The audience just sat and stared. Most operas have a moment when, however dull the spirits of the onlookers, the music gets through to some at least. These were impermeable.

Were we so awful? It seemed as good a performance as usual to me. Then I noted a new ingredient. It was our first performance to an audience in evening dress. There they were, sitting up straight and conscious of their elegance. Too trite an explanation? I don't think so. I like a relaxed audience. These people were stiff as starch. Many years later, most of our shows are to audiences dressed-up. So I always try to encourage my employers to give them a drink (better, several drinks) before we start. Alcohol is a great loosener of inhibitions.

Every audience contains people who would rather be elsewhere. Ours more than most, perhaps, because of the nature of our work. I used to calculate that the audience could be divided into thirds – one third who came for the opera, one third for the charity and one third for the house. And that's just the ticket-holders, any or all of which may well bring a partner or guest who for whatever reason has agreed to come against their better judgement. Bryan and I watch them, their faces lined with impenetrable gloom, glancing anxiously at their watches (in Act 1!) and trying to conceal their longing for bed, for the television, for anything other than Pavilion Opera!

I do try to include items for these unfortunates – some dancing, perhaps, a good fight, or some pretty girls. If we do our job properly, we should be able to find something for everyone. German dialogue stupefies some, although from personal experience I have always found one can follow most

The man who went to sleep
in the Front Row.

conversations abroad, if one watches the faces of those talking and listening. The camaraderie of laughter is quite powerful.

The paradox is this: on those nights when one or two singers are not at their best, when the timing seems awry, those are the times when audiences seem as enthusiastic as any. Again, I think it is the heroic effort made by the cast to recover from a setback which communicates itself to those who want them to succeed.

August 3

Don Giovanni at Beningborough; almost our sole surviving Trust employer, a last link with Ted Fawcett, our original Maecenas. The Trust's general and wholly understandable policy of cheap tickets does not square very easily with our need to pay good wages and offer reliability via a complete back-up team, employed to wait at home in case of emergencies.

But tonight is made possible by one of those who sponsor individual events, rather than us. Grace Steeplejacks have, in the past, given us direct sponsorship to renew the *Figaro* costumes, but tonight they're subsidizing the seats by paying money direct to Beningborough.

Panic when I arrived. We send out an identical letter to all the *Don Giovanni* houses, explaining the need for candles and smoke. Naturally, in a public building this needs head office authorization – two-fold here because the house has a fine collection lent by the National Portrait Gallery. The awful truth is that the Beningborough letter slipped through the net our end.

What to do? Give a second-rate performance, or try to get last-minute authorization? I just couldn't imagine the last scene without smoke. So I applied maximum pressure to the new administrator. He was a hero. He tried all the Trust officials – none were answering, so he took the decision himself. At the same time he made at least a dozen calls in connection with the National Portrait Gallery. With thirty minutes to go, their out-station director rang and I was able to reassure him that the smoke was harmless. If we could use candles in the Louvre, I argued, surely we could use them here. He agreed.

So on we went. The administrator turned off the fire alarm. Candles fluttered – the audience loved it. The acoustics at Beningborough are magnificently resonant and as the sunlight fades, the monumental columns in the Hall give it almost a feeling of an outdoor space – a courtyard, perhaps, in Rome or, as here intended, Seville.

Suddenly we reached the last great scene. Bryan thundered out the Commendatore's chords. The door opened – and a tidal wave of smoke overwhelmed us. The last thing I saw was the whitening face of an agonized man in the audience, and then we were engulfed. There was no chance of Bryan seeing the score on the keyboard. I just had time to grab the emergency torch I keep by the lighting board, but of course it made no difference at all. Yet he played on, totally confident, totally accurate. Alan boomed away somewhere out in the blackness, and then it was over. Thunderous applause. To be fair, even a single person clapping sounds pretty good at Beningborough. Anyway, the sponsors loved it.

'A great evening!' Mike Grace came over to shake my hand, dragging the downcast administrator with him.

'Now I know why I couldn't reach my boss,' the latter said glumly. 'He was in the audience.'

And I can guess which one he was, too.

August 5

Thorpe Tilney.

How nice to be at home. The Pavilion really comes to life when it is being used as intended. It was always a compromise between opera room and summer-house, and this month it gets a lot of use as the latter, although we don't have lunch out there as often as we used to. But for the next two days, *Figaro*, then *Don Giovanni*, at home. Bryan has his usual room, on the top floor, in Harry's old room. Noel and Helen have my room (because in the summer I sleep in a ground floor room with french windows giving on to the garden) and Alice gets the next most comfortable guest room. We've got eighteen in the house and five in the cottage, so it's pretty cramped by any standards. However careful our preparations, this is always the signal for the hot water system to break down!

Christine is in charge of all the arrangements – meals for ravenous singers, wine for the guests, an elaborate seating plan to squeeze the last possible person in, and the all-important sale of programmes.

Because our tour employers tend to go for the simplest options on the menus, lasagne, perhaps, or steak and kidney pie, here we always have joints of lamb, turkeys or duck, with treacle pudding or spotted dick, and poached salmon for the vegetarians.

August 6

'I gather Amy has been talking to you.'

This from Peter, as we waited for the cast supper to be served up. We were alone, as the others were still rehearsing.

'Mmm.' Our eyes locked. He's a determined character behind his genuine good humour.

'Did you give her any advice?' he demanded, rather belligerently.

'Yes,' I said. 'I advised her not to confide in her husband.'

'Well, she has,' he said. 'She has. And it's over.' He kicked a chair.

'Oi!' I said. 'Steady on.'

'She told him she loved me,' he said, his face getting red. 'How could he bear to touch her after that? Has he no pride?'

'She seemed very close to you this afternoon.'

'I've told her to make up her mind,' he almost shouted, but to himself. 'I'm not taking it in turns.'

'She's a Libra,' I said. 'They never make up their minds.'

'Good,' he said defiantly. 'I'll make it up for her, then.'

August 7

Figaro got some laughs for a change, but *Don Giovanni* nearly ended in tears. Bruce Rankin was singing Don Ottavio and decided to do the sword fight *à la* Frankie Howerd rather than Douglas Fairbanks. So while Roberto was slashing and lunging as practised, Bruce was holding his sword blade with three fingers and running round shrieking like a chicken without a head. He genuinely might have been killed, but the audience adored it.

Actually, I've never seen a chicken without a head, though I have to confess to a pigeon. Fathers who enthusiastically train their sons for bloodsports omit the intimate tragedies that follow. A wounded grouse can be killed by pressing in its skull above its eyes, a pheasant by holding the body with one hand, and stretching out its neck with two fingers clasped round its head. Years ago, as a school-boy, flighting pigeons in the snow, I had to finish off a wounded pigeon. I tried the grouse solution. Its eyes bulged in protest but nothing more. So I took its palpitating body with one hand, locked two fingers round its skull and to my horror the whole head came off, the corpse fluttered and danced round at my feet, blood spraying from the exposed and wrinkled hose of its neck. Will my sons complain in later life that I have tried so hard to spare them that sort of thing, or will they be grateful? Seated in a row, tonight, laughing at Bruce, they look wonderfully carefree.

August 9

Back to London, then up to Northamptonshire to collect
Alexander again. He and I are going to the Salzburg Festival
tomorrow, for three nights – an action-packed programme
before I take all the boys to Thorpe Tilney for three weeks of
swimming and scrabble.

August 14

Yesterday we saw *Figaro*, and tonight *Clemenza di Tito*. The
Figaro was frankly rather disappointing apart from a brilliant
performance by Diana Montague as Cherubino, and *Clemenza*
was a bit dull for Alexander. But we spent the day at
Herrenchiemsee, Ludwig of Bavaria's copy of Versailles (only
BIGGER), all alone on a misty island in the middle of a lake. We'd
hired a car, crossed into Germany and then got on a boat to get
there. It was superbly gilded but unmistakably nineteenth-
century. What a place for an opera!

August 15

Tonight was quite simply the best *Don Giovanni* I've ever seen.
So good, that I'm not sure I shall pay to see it on stage again for
a long long time, not until this image has faded. The Salzburg
scenery was high Baroque, forming and reforming into new and
wholly appropriate settings. Don Giovanni's myriad servants all
had white-painted faces, frizzy wigs and cherry-coloured livery,
including the three stage hands, two of whom were perched on
opposing balconies. It was sumptuous beyond belief and it had
Kathy Battle as an especially beguiling Zerlina. But the
knockout was the last scene.

One minute, there was the Don having the time of his life,

Viva buon vino, Vive le femine,
Sostegno e gloria d'umanità,

his toast 'to wine and women, The essence and glory of
mankind!', and the next minute, THE WHOLE OF THE BACK OF THE
STAGE WAS SPLIT ASUNDER AND THE STATUE WAS SEEN HURTLING
TOWARDS US THROUGH THE FIRMAMENT.

We were absolutely terrified.

Tumultuous applause, and richly deserved.

September 6

Everyone back in London for rehearsals after the holidays except
Emma who has been cruising in the Aegean and telegraphed that
she would be a day late. I didn't mind. She only has a minor part
here, whereas she is presumably taking the lead on board HMS
Goole.

Peter seems amazingly insouciant, but Amy has lost at least
half a stone, which she can ill afford. But she looks stunning,
with her great eyes staring out of a pale pale face.

She arrived alone. Twice she talked to Peter. Both times he
walked away.

'She's left her husband,' whispered Otto to me during the
second break.

I decided to keep out of the way, but just before the day
ended, she came up and said brightly, 'Can I walk back with
you?'

'Of course,' I said. I live five minutes' walk from the church
hall. She came up and I made her a cup of tea.

'So?'

'I've left Raoul.'

'I'm sorry.'

'There's no need to be. We weren't suited.'

This seemed admirably calm. But then she broke out in a thin wail: 'I've ruined his life. I've ruined his life.'

'Of course you haven't.'

'He says he wants to kill himself.'

'That's very silly of him.'

'Haven't you ever felt like that?' she demanded.

'Everyone does. Everyone gets over it.'

'Some people don't,' she said with almost a note of satisfaction.

I thought about Raoul. I couldn't remember very much about him, except that he looked gloomy. 'You can't run other people's lives.'

'Not even when you've promised in church?' Oh, Lord! What painful dilemmas we all face.

'Can you face another forty years with him?' I asked.

'NO!' It wasn't exactly a shout, more a public announcement.

'Well, then.' At least there were no children. But I felt, too late perhaps, that I was getting too closely connected with her decisions. Friends and employers have their duties and their natural impulses to listen and help. But a certain distance is prudent. Or is that selfish self-preservation?

We had some more tea. I distracted her by talking about next year's roles, and sent her home in a minicab.

September 12

Golly. Last week was wall-to-wall *Don Giovanni*s. Caroline and Helen took it in turns with Donna Anna, and Arthur did one of the Dons, but Noel did all six Leporellos. He's looking rather pale – but then, he always does, and it's his choice, admittedly wholeheartedly backed by Bryan and me.

Tonight it's *Don Pasquale* at a music society. There's a scene when Norina overturns all the furniture, shouting 'This house is in a disgraceful state!' It's always risky – tonight Caroline picked up the quill and threw it in the air. It decided to be a dart and flew into the audience, hitting a woman in the chest. The audience howled; I was rather worried – that's not what she bought a ticket for. The first night ever, at Thorpe Tilney, Rebecca flung a book into the air; it landed on my vicar, and turned out to be the *Apocrypha* (well – it could have been worse). At Aske, Helen landed a cloth on Leon Brittan's head (it was assumed to be deliberate – I said, 'Well, you try doing it!'), and at Mellerstain Susan flung a cushion and caught the piano light (a small Regency electric candelabra) which smashed onto Bryan's lap in a cloud of sparks. But no one has yet equalled Ann Liebeck at the Watts Gallery. She threw both cushions into the air with a wild shriek and the whole of the top of her dress dropped off.

The Diva shows more than she intends

September 13

So why does opera sometimes fail? The first reason is a simple one – lack of confidence.

How, must the uninitiated feel at the prospect of entering a vast throng of opera experts (everyone else is an opera expert when you go for the first time) who may turn round and stare at you if you go to sleep/laugh/clap in the wrong place/don't clap in the right place. It is an intimidating experience – until you've done it. Then it seems as natural as walking into a restaurant.

Certainly the message of the last ten years has been that the more opera you put on, the more people will gradually get used to the idea and feel relaxed about coming.

Films and television have done a lot to help, by reminding people that operas are often little more than eighteenth- and nineteenth-century musicals – with lots of popular tunes. Just listen to television advertisements: are they trying to sell a car? or an aeroplane ticket? or football seats? Very often, that catchy tune is by Verdi, or Mozart, or Rossini.

Another reason for opera's isolation, which I can readily appreciate, is the danger of being bored. I have been more bored by bad opera performances than by any other activity. How one longs for the blessed oblivion of sleep. Or the chance to slip away! But no – the noise is too great, the heat too oppressive, one's hostess too near. Two or three occasions like that, and a newcomer to opera will decide to spend the money on something else. It's not a *moderate* form of entertainment. It is either immoderately enthralling or, when badly played or badly directed or badly cast, immoderately alienating. I say 'cast', because the responsibility for a singer rests on his or her employer's aesthetic judgement. If they sing a role badly or inaudibly, they shouldn't have been given the job. A voice is a voice, subject only to ill-health or abnormal dottiness.

But the reason most often given for opera not being more popular – the price of the tickets – is a false one. Opera has always been expensive: if you have three sets, a medium-sized orchestra of sixty, ten principals, a chorus of twenty-four, plus stage hands, front-of-house, and administration, there are rarely fewer than a hundred and twenty people employed on the show. And that's a lot more than most musicals, though about par for an extended pop concert tour. Yes! A ticket to a first-class pop concert is about the same as the true cost of an opera ticket (that is, if the opera ticket were to include paying back the subsidy which the taxpayer currently contributes.) Nothing élitist about pop concerts. People buy tickets in their thousands because they *want* to go. It was the same with opera in the nineteenth century.

York had an opera house; Newcastle had *three*, one of them built by an Italian architect specially imported for the job. I bet Lloyd George's budgets didn't cover 'provision of Italian and German operas at public expense'.

The law of the market is unbreakable. Scotch whisky costs a lot more in Tokyo than in Tomintoul – but if you want it, you pay. Indeed, at grand Japanese parties, nothing less can be served.

September 14

If there is a single major explanation for most poor opera performances, it is perhaps lack of rehearsal.

We spend sixty sessions (that is, 180 hours) on each new opera, seventy if it is to be performed with an orchestra, who will have started rehearsals separately. This is on the strict understanding that every member of the cast, from the leading principal to the understudy of the most invisible member of the chorus, knows the words *and* music by heart before we start. And of course it would be better if we had longer, though there is a point where the work begins to go stale without the extra impetus of a live audience.

Some major performers speak of being given two or three days' rehearsal if they are lucky. Of course, on a stage, the possible moves are greatly reduced. And the star will often be giving his or her standard interpretation of the role, whereas the minor characters will have been rehearsed for longer by the house producer. Problems can arise if these two approaches are not compatible.

When Beethoven's work first astounded a musical world unused to his innovative vocabulary, one of the problems was that hardly anyone could play it. No wonder the audiences were so confused, faced with incompetent renditions of such complicated pieces as his posthumous quartets. But rehearsals cost money – a circular problem. Similarly, in the orchestras there is a mischievous custom called 'depping' or deputizing. By this means a player can sub-contract some of his sessions of employment (usually during rehearsals) to another player, often making a profit on the arrangement, while taking up better-paid employment elsewhere. You can reach a position, therefore, where the orchestra playing at the performance is not necessarily wholly or even largely the orchestra that has been paid to rehearse. This is often true of major orchestral tours, where the most important ingredient is the brand name.

I mustn't knock the system too much. It helps us to recruit and retain our excellent players, whose regular work is elsewhere. When they come to Pavilion, deputies take over their places there. But the principle is not good.

September 15

Yesterday morning I flew to Madrid to look at the Palace Hotel. Phyllida has taken a contract from them for early October. I'm not worried, as they assured her they have a tall room often used for concerts. But I want to see it, just to be sure.

Like Solomon before the Queen of Sheba, the half had not been told to me. A colossal room, the main part defined by a circle of double columns; on these rests a curving dome of Art Deco glass, perhaps a hundred feet in diameter. Impossible to imagine a better setting – acoustics, architectural drama, and masses of space (they want to invite three hundred), all combined with the resources of a major hotel.

Then we went to lunch. The man in charge, Luis Soler, had given me some sherry upstairs. Now we waded our way through a great communal dish of smoked ham, striped crimson and white between lean and fat, and meltingly tender. Next came the famous spanish baby eels, mounds and mounds of them, washed down by a flinty white wine; a *fritto misto* of all the varieties with which Spanish fish markets abound – red, blue, grey and white – and a delicious salad.

I sat back, sighing. Food is one of life's great pleasures. I think it was the sight, out of the corner of my eye, of a waiter bringing up two bottles of red Burgundy which alerted me that we hadn't finished. I always think that sucking pig should be served off-stage, as it were; I also have reservations about restaurants that present the lobster still struggling – one may not wish to look one's lunch in the eyes. Nevertheless, this was a revelation to anyone familiar with school pork. I ate the cheese almost without thinking: Luis was speculating on the right wine for the *bombe glacé* a thoughtful Phyllida had recommended as my favourite. Clearly we would be here for most of the afternoon.

'A glass of brandy?' I heard him saying later.

'Why not?'

A *trolley* of bottles swam smoothly into view.

'Hine? Delamain? Hennessy?' I stared at the surreal array. 'Martell? Otard? San Sebastian?'

'A small glass of Hine, please.' I was articulating carefully. A brimming beaker was put in front of me.

What a host!

I hardly remember the drive to the airport, and had to be shaken awake at Gatwick. Luckily my liver is pretty resilient. But I'm not looking forward to the drive to Wales tomorrow.

September 17

Barmouth. A long-standing love-affair. Well, we love it, and they are kind enough to keep employing us. It's a pretty white town perched between the mountains and the sea on the north Wales coast. The drive here is long but spectacular, with plunging ravines and tall foamy waterfalls.

The first year we came I was still a member of a curious body, now reformed, called the Nurses and Midwives Whitley Council. In one corner were the Regional representatives (that's us), in the other the Unions, divided into two camps: one, the Royal College of Nurses and ditto of Midwives (also us), the other NUPE (them) rather half-heartedly backed by COHSE and others. The arena was refereed by permanent officials of the Department (that is to say, the men who actually made the money decisions). Our job was to try to divide up their cake by agreement with the Unions. My distinction between us and them is made as dividing those who wanted to get better conditions tomorrow but would settle for responsible management today (us), and those who wanted to demand more money with menaces, the strike weapon (them). They were chaired by a Welshman of great charm and wit called David Williams, of COHSE.

So imagine my surprise when I looked out at the audience during our performance to see, lounging in the converted theatre's only box, in imperial isolation, the General Secretary of NUPE!

In the interval I sought out our employer at Barmouth, the indefatigable Mrs Repath.

'Am I going mad, or is that Mr Fisher in the box?'

'Oh, yes,' she said. 'He's our prime patron.'

'Indeed? Does he live near here, then?'

'Yes,' she said. 'He has a castle this side of the estuary.'

Gulp.

And the next year I found myself, with Noel and Helen, billeted with him. I'm bound to say that he and his wife made us tremendously welcome, and memories of the 1978/9 winter of discontent seemed far away.

In fact, there are similar problems within Pavilion Opera. Nurses were, eventually, given a say in the general management of hospitals, a seat on hospital boards. Where once there had been an administrator, more or less cued by the chief doctor, now there was a management board – an administrator, a doctor, an engineer, an accountant and a nurse. And if all those people sat round a table together, it was argued, they should all be paid the same.

Why? Because, it was further argued, a person's status is dictated by his or her salary. The others will not listen to the nurse if he or she is paid less. This was not an argument that greatly appealed to our side, where members served voluntarily! – although it did furtively cross my mind that it might have some substance at Whitley. But the real flaw is this. Once you accept that premiss, you are then faced with the counter-argument: we, the nurse, doctor, et cetera, are all paid the same, but how is this equitable if I manage five times more staff than *he* does; or if I have responsibility for a budget ten times to one *she* deals with? And so on. Quite persuasive, is it not? That's what keeps most union negotiators in business.

In Pavilion Opera, the similarity arises as regards roles. One singer may be coping with three or four major roles, a second may only have chorus parts, or minor roles. Should the first singer be paid more because he or she is doing greater, higher-profile work? Or the second more because he or she is not doing what he or she *wants*, but rather the humbler (but no less essential) parts that are vital to the opera? Common sense suggests the first, market forces the second. And they all, figuratively speaking, sit round the same table. We are a team.

It's rare to meet anyone who thinks they're paid enough. But quite a lot of nurses will say privately that they love the work and appreciate the (relatively) colossal increases (60 per cent in one year, through the Clegg commission) of the late 1970s and early 1980s, combined with the shorter working week which their representatives pressed for so enthusiastically.

But not NUPE. 'Ten per cent of nothing is nothing,' was their leader's ringing cry. Sixty per cent of nothing is also nothing. I thought it a very promising approach.

September 19

Back from Wales, and at last the dreaded performance of *Don Giovanni* at North Mymms. I had decided not to go, and accepted for a party instead, but in the end I decided to pop down for half an hour. I was worried that the cast might be bullied and I wanted to meet John Elliott, if only to thank him for letting me stay in his Melbourne flat.

I got there at four o'clock to find everyone comfortably settled in. The room looked fine. The chairs were perfectly laid out.

'Sorry about the acoustics,' I said to Bryan.

He looked surprised 'Why? They're fine.'

I clapped my hands. Nice and resonant! I must have had an off day.

The cast's meal appeared. It looked delicious.

A nice woman in pink brought me the cheque. 'Is John Elliott here yet?' I asked.

'No,' she said, 'he's had to fly back to Australia. Will you join us for a drink afterwards?'

'No,' I said, now regretfully. 'I'm not staying. I just wanted to see that all is well.'

'Just come for the money, I suppose,' said the chairman, walking past.

Bryan rang after the show to say that it went really well.

September 21

Rigoletto at Stoke Manor, one of the houses where we can all stay with our hosts.

Another long talk with Amy, circular and depressing. There are, we've all met them, people who truly love themselves – the ideal of self-contained reciprocated affection. For the rest of us, the search is on. No wonder most literature, most opera, is focused on love. It is the absorbing interest of most adults, certainly of most artists. And for each of those alone who seek to be a partner, there are as many coupled who seek to be apart.

'Tout comprendre, c'est tout pardonner.' Oh yes! How often we long to be spared that understanding which absolves the betrayal, leaving us impaled on the icy splinters of indifference, with love lacerated yet so painfully alive.

I was just dozing off when I heard Amy's voice through the communicating door. She and Peter had the adjoining bedroom.

'But I don't want it to end. DO YOU HEAR?'

I could hear Peter frantically urging her to keep her voice down. 'I DON'T CARE WHO BLOODY HEARS. I DON'T WANT IT TO END!'

There was the sound of a smack and a scuffle. Then silence. And then moans. I tried burying my head under the pillow. It only helped a little. My mind was full of my own problems, and it was nearly dawn before I drifted into sleep.

September 22

'I hope I didn't disturb you last night Freddie.' It was Amy. She sidled up to me just before rehearsal today.

'Disturb me?' I smiled at her. She had black rings under her eyes and looked delightfully raffish.

'Peter and I were arguing . . .' She looked up at me carefully.

'I slept like a log. You'll have to do more than argue if you want to wake *me* up.'

Her face closed up again, and with a satisfied nod she walked over to join the others by the piano. Jeans suit her – she has a decided swagger.

September 23

Today we had a Pavilion Opera committee meeting. This is the nearest thing we have to a policy debate. The committee consists of three dedicated friends. Marcus Edwards, once married to my late and much-loved sister, is our Chairman. By day he is a judge, but by night he and his wife Sandra work hard to help promote our work overseas. He is flanked by Rosalind Hanbury, an employer, who represents the consumer interests of those who use us to raise money, and Paul Sandilands, a City sponsor who advises on the financial implications. To these, Bryan, Christine (UK bookings), Phyllida (overseas), Caroline Llewellyn (auditions and sponsorship) and I present reports for discussion, decision and implementation.

Eight years of Health Authority Committees have made me wary of such gatherings – but this one works well. It gives us all a chance to stand back and consider the annual events. And because we are all active in the work and no one is a supernumerary, no one listens silently without an idea to contribute. Today we concentrated on a future production, *Cenerentola* (neither Bryan nor I warm to Rossini, but it is a perfect opera for our style), insurance policy overseas (no to personal effects), problems (difficult employers) and the *Don Pasquale* costumes. The producer likes these tatty – indeed, he told Colin to tear them more to make them look worse. But the audience think them dreary and don't understand that a point (that the Don is filthy and unkempt) is being made. I have agreed that Colin will make some smart new dresses for the heroine, Norina, out of the contingency budget for next year.

September 24

Powderham. Usually our furthest point west. It's such a wonderful castle – grimly fortified outside, gaily decorated within. I arrived early to be told that there was a Trustees' meeting in the wing and any problems would be sorted out when that was over.

The first problem was thick smoke billowing out of a second-floor window. I rushed to the wing, couldn't get through the first door, so hammered on the second. Eventually I pushed past a startled secretary to alert the Trustees that their deliberations were likely to be rather pointless unless someone rang the Fire Brigade. They were remarkably relaxed. 'Oh, that's my mother's cooker again,' said the heir. 'It's always doing that.'

I went off for my annual cup of tea with Colonel Delforce, their fiercely loyal factotum. This is our sixth performance in the Music Room, fitted up by the Lord Courtenay of the day (in whose bedroom at Fonthill William Beckford was unlucky enough to be caught). Not only does it have a concealed stage but, even better, there is a spring-loaded trapdoor – from which he used to pop up, smothered in sequins, to amuse his tenants. The only snag is a heating grille in the main doorway – each year first the door bolt gets stuck in it, and then a regular attender's stick. Bryan and I have come to look forward to these nostalgic moments.

Lord and Lady Devon sit in two colossal gilded *fauteuils* while the rest of the audience perch on plastic chairs. What is nice is that, far from being resented, this is absolutely accepted. They are kind to us always – tonight was no exception. Bottles of wine and a feast of sandwiches after the show.

September 25

I picked up the latest overseas post for Phyllida *en route* to collect Harry from school to visit some architectural sites for his A-level studies. It's nice to find myself learning from him, now.

While he was sketching Archer's Baroque pavilion, all that is left of the Duke of Kent's great garden at Wrest Park, the house having been remodelled as a dotty Russian palazzo in the nineteenth century, I read the replies from my trawl of British cultural attachés. Some were supportive (Tokyo, Brussels), others less so. Our man in Rome wrote crushingly, 'I think you may have more success *north* of the Alps'. Like Hannibal, I long to deliver my reply in person.

There was worse to come. Eagerly tearing open the envelope from Bonn, I was met with this: 'As you know, there are no country houses in Germany'. Germany? No country houses? Arolsen, Brühl, the Residenz of Würzburg, Pommersfelden, the Nymphenburg, Linderhof, Herrenchiemsee, Neuschwanstein; Wolfsgarten, where I stayed last year, in its impenetrable forest still scattered with ancient rides for driving the game towards firing loop-holes in the wall of the castle; and that's just a start. Germany, almost the mother of the Baroque. Germany, where every crag on the Rhine is topped by a towering fortress. Is this man's culture so blinkered by suburban prejudice that he cannot see the great German palaces even when they surround him on every side?

'What's the matter, Dad?' It was Harry, back with his sketchbook, looking at me with a worried air.

'I want to scream,' I said.

'Okay,' he said. 'I'll just do one more drawing, then.'

September 30

Figaro at Stowe. In the back corridor I found Peter sitting on an old laundry basket. He had his head in his hands. I put a hand on his shoulder, uncertain what to say but wanting to show some slight sign of support.

'Oh, God!' He lifted a tear-drenched face. 'I don't mind being rejected myself. But it's awful what I've done to Amy.'

'Budge up.' He shifted on the basket and I sat down beside him.

'She says' – he gave a great sigh, and then tried again – 'she says she prays every night to be allowed to die.'

'Well, she looked pretty chirpy in the dressing roon just now.'

'Yes,' he said. 'She's such a great actress.'

'Fifteen minutes!' Bruce Carter's voice echoed down the stairwell. 'This is your fifteen-minute call.'

'Damn!' I said, getting up. 'I've still got to check the gangways. You coming up?'

'In a minute,' he said. 'I'll be there.'

October 2

Back in Madrid, but this time with the *Rigoletto* cast, and my second son, Alexander.

Rigoletto is one of the perfect operas: a strong story (based on Victor Hugo's play *Le Roi s'Amuse*), and endless good tunes. Susan is singing Gilda, Arthur Rigoletto, and Bruce Rankin is singing the Duke, which means we shall be doing a longer version than is usually heard, because he can manage *both* verses of the cabaletta.

Luis' team has transformed the room, isolating it from the rest of the Palace Hotel with heavy velvet curtains, and filling it with plants, candelabra and very grand flower arrangements on plinths between the pillars.

Our rooms all have fruit and wine, there is *carte blanche* in the Grill, the singers are, predictably, in a sunny mood and eager to sing their best. In the afternoon Alexander and I saw Bryan and both Bruces in the Prado, all congregating at the exquisite Bruegel de Velours flower paintings. I took Alexander to see the rather overblown Rubens room and then on to the Goya country scenes – there they all were again!

We started late so as not to exclude some delayed guests. As usual, this rather damped those who had got there on time. But they soon warmed up in the Act 2 duets, and by the end they stood and cheered, which was nice.

The supper, to which we were all invited, had one common ingredient: caviare. There was caviare and soup, caviare and salmon, caviare and blinis, caviare in *mille-feuilles*, caviare in vodka sorbet and (best of all) caviare by itself.

Then they brought in a massive chocolate creation – a chocolate grand piano and a group of large chocolate figures with the faces (can you believe this?) of the cast, faithfully reproduced from their photographs. I've never seen anything like it before, and probably never will again. The chocolate man had been brought over from Italy with his team. He was justly proud.

October 3

Back to London. Most of the singers have brought their chocolate figures with them. Those put in the baggage compartments melted!

October 8

Oh dear – Blenheim, here we come. Christine rang this morning as I was approaching Oxford.

'Now, don't forget,' she said.

'Forget what?'

'What you said about Blenheim.'

'What did I say?' I was totally foxed.

'You said that you were going to keep calm whatever the Comptroller did or said, because it is a beautiful building and you're making a good profit.'

'Oh, God!' I'd forgotten all about the Comptroller!

But it is fun to work with the orchestra and it's especially popular with the singers, who feel somehow more respectable when they are competing with the brass rather than being supported by a single piano.

The palace was looking magnificent. There's no grading for Vanbrugh's masterpieces: Blenheim, Castle Howard, Seaton Delaval – each one has its separate claim to be the best. But Blenheim was looking pretty good this morning – glowing a warm gold in the sharp sunlight with the water flashing and rippled by the wind. A perfect set for Valhalla.

To my great surprise, everything seemed in order. The changing room (for fifty of us) was warm and supplied with tea and coffee machines. The chairs were laid out rather oddly, but I soon got them in order. The Comptroller was all smiles. False alarm? I don't think so; I'm still glad I got here very early.

I lunched in the village. The little pub was almost too dark for me to read my book, but there was plenty to worry about. Sadly, Helen and Alice are both moving on in December, and Susan is still making up her mind. Caroline Friend is staying, so are Alan, Enid, Noel and Blair. Roberto will if I can renew his work permit, Bruce Rankin will if he has a bit more time to think about it. The whole backstage team – Bruce Carter, Nicky Whitsun-Jones, Matt, Colin, Nicky Jackson – have signed on *en masse*. Plus Bryan: conductor, pianist, musical director, coach, adviser and friend. So, the outlook is pretty rosy for the new season.

Back to our current coalface – now even deeper gold, with dark blue shadows etched across its façade.

> Change and decay in all around I see
> But Thou, who changest not, abide with me.

Blenheim has something of the dignity of a cathedral, with its long vaulted corridors, booming now with the resonance of the great boilers that keep it so warm. Certainly no other building expresses better the apparent invulnerability of Britain's past. Whatever their private concerns, the members of this family preserve their base with colossal *éclat*.

This impression was slightly eroded when I reached the Hall

to find that doors to the Saloon, and the newly-restored gilt console table, are being shrouded in – plastic!

'Why are you doing that?' I asked mildly.

'His Grace's orders. He's worried that they might get damaged.'

'It does look rather odd,' I observed.

'Maybe,' he said, sticking more plastic onto the gleaming mahogany of the door.

Everyone told me that the Hall's acoustics would be disastrous. But the hand-clapping test had suggested otherwise, and so it proved.

A piano would have sounded stark, but as soon as Bryan walked in, bowed to the Royal Guest of Honour and took up his baton, the room was filled with soft music – if it echoed round the pillars and drifted up and down the arcades, that only added to its mystery. And when the trumpets and the horns sounded up to the roof, where Marlborough's battle banners were flapping in the currents of hot air, I could see the audience surrendering to the occasion.

It was very much a Sotheby's evening, and their chairman gave a generous speech at the end. All seemed well and I said goodbye to those involved, thanking the Comptroller for making it all such a pleasure. He replied effusively.

But before I got to London, Colin rang in tears to say that no sooner had I left than the Comptroller had returned to shout at him. I had dropped my guard. I should have stayed.

October 9

The start of the new auditions for next year. Caroline Llewellyn has had over 200 applications from singers. The first thing to do is to sift through for past disasters. We have three marks – 1 means first-class, suitable for principal roles; 2 means fine for an understudy and may improve, so can be heard every two or three years; 3 means unemployable. Most get a 3. But now we've had to add a special mark – NAUAC (never again under *any* circumstances). This denotes those hardy annuals who try to slip back in; today we had two, both using new names, which it is very difficult to screen against. We just grin and suffer. No one here who is better than the existing group.

Dinner with Linda and David Heathcoat Amory to celebrate, belatedly, David's great success in getting Roberto a work permit to sing Don Giovanni. I had Rosalind Hanbury on one side so we started planning *Tales of Hoffman* for next year. The music is so brass-bandy that I'm hoping to introduce a little military band – an itinerant group (rather like us) who happen to be playing in Luther's tavern (Act 1) and then turn up again in Venice where Giulietta, the most celebrated *grande horizontale* of her day, is performing a cabaret (Act 2). It's so nice to have a chance to talk ideas over, rather than having them banging about inside one's own head like so many trapped birds.

October 10

What a flight! Even direct to Tokyo, with Virgin, it seemed endless. They showed us two videos and, a nice touch, sent round an ice-cream lady in the 'interval'. Choc-ices all round! There was a huge bus, very luxurious, to meet us, and a bevy of people from Hermès, our employers. This hotel is spectacular – brand new and very high-tech. Tonight we are being taken to a restaurant by the Hermès chief, Monsieur Kato, who came to Attingham two years ago.

October 11

An amazing evening last night. We were all taken in a series of cars through the brightly-lit streets. Eventually, down a tiny alley, we reached a wooden house in a large garden. Masses of drinks were laid out on a table by a pool – whisky, champagne, saké, whatever. Then we were taken into the house where we all (about twenty-five including our hosts) sat on the floor with a middle-aged geisha between each pair. There were lots of courses, all delicious, and my geisha, who spoke excellent English, kept filling up my cup of warm spicy saké. It was very reviving. There was a sudden burst of laughter from down the table. Apparently the geisha looking after Nick Heath, the new tenor, was fingering his beard and picking bits of fish out of it! Then there was some music, and we were all handed a song sheet to sing a Japanese folksong. Then more tea, more food, more saké. I could hardly walk when I left, though I *hope* this was the result of a long flight followed by sitting on the floor for a couple of hours.

October 12

Noel, Nick and Susan went off to a Kabuki theatre today, and Bruce, Bryan and Enid went to Disneyland. I am trying to write a novel about an auction house without suggesting either Sotheby's or Christie's. I've found a corner on the twentieth floor where I can look out over the city and smoke in peace.

October 13

We're still recovering – the singers, that is – from dehydration on the flight. Phyllida and I went to Hermès' head office today to check through tomorrow's arrangements. It's all very precise. We had sent them photographs of the props needed – those provided appear to be identical. Perhaps they have been made specially? Tonight they took us to a restaurant where everything was cooked in front of us – even live shrimps.

'Oh, look!' said the exquisite Japanese girl on my right, pointing at a wriggling crustacean. 'He's waving! He's calling for help!' I looked at her shining eyes – she really was frighteningly pretty. But it was too much for Alan; he said he was tired, and withdrew until the next course.

October 14

The French Embassy is very modernistic. I arrived at three to find the room exactly as when I had first seen it two years ago. Panic.

'Are you worried?' asked the Hermès girl.

'Yes,' I said, looking at my watch.

'It will all be ready,' she said, and sure enough an absolute army of men appeared – perhaps fifty – and by 4.30 three hundred chairs were in place, all the lighting and all the props. Very impressive.

October 16

Heavens above! Another wonderful evening – everything perfectly organized, and tonight the party of parties – I asked Jean-Louis Hermès and Monsieur Kato back to my room for a party with the cast. I also asked three of the Hermès girls, but protocol prevented them joining. Trays of saké and half a dozen bottles of wine kept us going for two or three hours. Eventually our hosts went to bed, whereupon Nick and Alan gave a demonstration of sumo wrestling culminating in our chasing a naked Nick down the corridor with jugs of iced water. I *think* we were alone on this floor – I certainly hope so. It's hardly worth going to bed. We have to be up at five to catch the Tokyo connection to London.

October 19

Back to Paris – this time for a very grand Embassy party.
Everyone is on their tiptoes, worrying about security and
timing. Ben, the Embassy butler, is superbly calm, effortlessly
supervising his extra staff. Are you picturing a stately figure,
bald and pear-shaped? Despite long service Ben is under thirty,
slight but straight, with a perfect mixture of poise and
helpfulness.

'Everything all right, Freddie?'

'It's all fine.' This is the fourth show we've done together.

'Well, if you want anything, just let me know.' He walks off,
followed by two anxious footmen. As if he hadn't better things
to do than worry about us! By six o'clock I was so nervous I had
to walk down to the Comédie Française and back, puffing acrid
smoke and stopping for a *citron pressé* near the Madeleine. French
women may not be prettier, but they try much harder than the
English. This was a last-minute booking – a cabaret performance
of Act 2 of *Fledermaus* – so I have sent most of the cast on to
Boston: Alice, Enid, Blair, Phyllida and the others. I've got
Bryan, Colin, Noel and Bruce Carter here, together with those
not going to America, including Caroline, Stefan, and Susan.

We were planning to start at 7.30. Then there was a hitch so it
was put back to 7.45. I came down to check with Bruce, to be
grabbed by a frantic aide.

'They're all in. You've got to start!' Bruce ran up to get the

Calming the impresario's
NERVES

cast and I slipped in behind the curtains and sat down beside the piano. The audience stared.

And we waited.

Five minutes – nothing.

I was trying to keep calm.

Ten minutes – the first trickle of perspiration began to make its way past my ear. Why on earth wouldn't they talk among themselves? I decided to chance a nonchalant glance across to the Fergussons. Aaaargh! I found myself staring straight into the eyes of the guests of honour. To their right Sir Ewen raised his eyebrows.

I raised mine. There was nothing I could do, but I felt the unmistakable wave of scalding blush turning my face purple. Another five minutes. This was intolerable! What on . . . In came Bryan, gales of applause, the first notes, a shriek from the go-go dancer and we were away. 'Amy's zip broke,' he whispered.

I'm afraid the high point had nothing to do with our work.

There's a moment when Caroline, disguised as a Hungarian Countess with one of Colin's favourite ostrich feathers in her head-dress, withdraws from the action. By chance there was a chair empty at the end, next to the French Prime Minister, a friendly man with tight, curly hair.

She sat down beside him. People cope with this in different ways. Some enjoy it and play up generously; some hate it and turn black with rage and embarrassment; others overdo it and start a conversation – though you might think that a just desert. Anyhow, the Prime Minister was perfect; he smiled amiably, looked her up and down (that got a laugh), and all might have been well. But she has a bit of stage business where she looks round the room . . . the audience started laughing. I looked over: her feather was tickling his hair and he was doing a good job staying cool and smiling, but with little lines of unease about the eyes.

Worse was to come. Now the feather got caught in his curls,

so that Caroline became aware that something was wrong. Her smile became slightly forced. Not so the rest of us. The more perplexed the Ambassadorial front row became (because they couldn't see), the funnier it was for the rest of us. Suddenly Caroline came to a decision, and stood up. If the feather had stayed in the Prime Minister's hair, I don't think Bryan could have carried on. Luckily it stayed with Caroline, and the evening ended with a dance.

October 20

We five had to be up at six to catch the first flight to London to connect with the morning flight to Boston. It was sad to arrive there so depleted – two years ago here, with our hosts Lucy and Barclay Tittmann, we had all had a snowfight in the dark with Alice and Blair leading the indeterminate teams. But not today – and there was Lucy, with a lovely smile, waiting for us at the Customs gate.

'You must be dead,' she said, kissing us all. 'Come and get in the cars. We're all having an early supper together.'

October 21

Oh, no! If the others feel as awful as I do, what will it be like? Luckily, they didn't. And I soon revived after one of Lucy's spectacular breakfasts. Having six children may be some preparation for having an opera company descend on you, but I still admire people who cope as calmly and with as much genuine kindliness as the Tittmanns. Barclay even smuggled some Havana cigars from Canada for me. To appreciate the real impact of this, I have to tell you that they *hate* people to smoke in their house. So why do I do it? Because it is impossible to refuse such straightforward generosity.

210

October 22

Don Giovanni at the Tittmanns' house, an ingeniously-designed high-tech bungalow built round an eighteenth-century two-storey barn, went so well that I was grateful this was nearly the end of the season. They laughed uproariously at all Don Giovanni's jokes – there must have been a lot of Italian-speakers. Roberto was thrilled. What on earth would happen if we went back to a dour Hexham audience now?

Lucy drove us down to Wilmington with her sculptress daughter Sally. We stopped to look at Yale and then at Lyndhurst, the Goulds' ethereal Gothick mansion overlooking the Hudson. It is glitteringly pale outside, darkly sinister inside, with doors opening on unexpected angles and a pervasive atmosphere of brooding menace. Could Shirley Jackson have seen it before she wrote her masterpiece *The Haunting of Hill House*, of which it was said 'Whatever walked there, walked alone'.

October 23

On to Wilmington, Delaware. Sue Ward, Annie Jones and Willy Prickett have formed a group of opera enthusiasts, rather like Rosie Taylor's group at Cricket. They planned tonight's performance at a series of parties, everyone in the audience went to one of several big dinner parties afterwards, and there was a really positive feeling among everyone involved. I had been in a panic about the acoustic tiles. But it went very well.

October 25

Another lesson not to compromise. Yesterday we hired a charabanc to take us to the Roundhill Club, Greenwich. A nice audience, but the opera was amost inaudible because of the bigger, better acoustic tiles. Unlike Wilmington, the room was covered with the beastly things. The audience were courteous, but I should have refused to perform in that room.

Just as the cast were taking their bow, a self-appointed spokesman stood up and addressed them in mid curtain call. This is always a mistake, but stuck behind the piano there was nothing I could do.

'Nor must we forget', he boomed past the bemused singers, 'my good friend Frank Stogpot.' This, pointing at me, which cheered the singers up.

Today I've reached San Francisco to stay for a couple of days with Paul and Marina du Saillant. I saw the others off at Kennedy airport at ten o'clock. A long day, but with time to see the Rodin sculpture garden at Stanford University: they are also the saviours of Harlaxton, Lincolnshire's grandest nineteen-century palace, which the University bought when it was threatened by neglect.

October 26

Up early (not difficult considering the time change) to go with Marina to see the giant redwoods. They are beyond description – Nature's skyscrapers, and emotionally very moving in their peaceful isolation. What must this coast have looked like once? She says that they must feed off the mist, since the rains are so irregular.

She and Paul have just been staying with a genuine anchorite, the Diogenes of northern California. He has constructed a house out of giant barrels, sliced and joined together to provide a complete home, with kitchen and bathroom.

'But where did you stay?' I asked.

'In the guest-barrel.'

The French Consul has, as he promised, arranged a great lunch party for me to meet potential employers. A press interview, then a quick trip to Filoli, a possible house. There's hardly time to turn round, but with no performance it seems luxuriously relaxed. In the evening we went to *Khovanschina* at the Opera House. By coincidence, Nicolai Ghiaurov, whom I'd seen so many years ago in Paris, was singing Khovansky. A happy day.

October 28

We spent most of my last morning in City Lights, San Francisco's answer to Heywood Hill. Then a glimpse of the El Grecos in the Legion of Honour Museum and back to the airport. I could have stayed for months!

Five years ago in America, I was rather inclined to be surprised at the level of resources employed – for example, the Musical Director at Boston said they couldn't afford understudies if they were to have at least one international star, and when I saw *Wiener Blut* in Washington there were only twenty-three musicians in the pit. Did it sound thin only because we are used to bombast? But then I thought about it from a different perspective. After all, when Liszt was Kapellmeister at Weimar, scene of so many famous premières, he had thirty-five in his orchestra, twenty-three in his chorus, and four dancers for ballet. Indeed, for the world première of *Lohengrin*, the orchestra was increased to thirty-eight! (Five first violins, six seconds, three violas, four cellos, three basses, two flutes, two oboes, two clarinets, two bassoons, four horns, two trumpets, a trombone, a tuba and a kettledrummer.) Not ideal, of course not – but it was acceptable, then. So much have times changed that when we used a slightly larger orchestra, more violins and trombones, for *Don Giovanni* in Northampton, it was described by a local critic, *de haut en bas*, as a 'small band'.

A little modesty in one's demands does not necessarily forswear musicality. The Met, unsubsidized, deploys a cast of thousands, with a vast orchestra to match – because it can afford to. But when the Leipzig theatre orchestra under Küstren (1820s) reached thirty-three, he proudly wrote of them as being 'as complete as one finds them in the best Court theatres'. And, to put us all in perspective, they were giving two hunded and eighty-three performances a year of works by Gluck, Mozart, Beethoven, Weber, Cimarosa and Rossini.

So what next? After orchestras specially composed of antediluvian instruments played at unusual tempi, what about smaller theatres with casts and orchestras more accurately reflecting the original performances? After all, who wants to sit in the thirtieth row of *anything*?

October 29

Moscow at last, with *Figaro*. We flew in last night. By good fortune it's half-term so I have Harry with me. We're sharing the same room at the Embassy as I had before – looking straight over the Moscow river at the Kremlin.

Tonight we were all taken to the Circus. It was SPECTACULAR. The most interesting part was the way they were able to drop the whole arena hydraulically and replace it with another, in this case a giant pool complete with islands, filled with gymnastic girls swimming in perfect unison.

'I know that look,' said Noel. 'What are we in for now?' 'Well,' I pointed out, 'Wagner always said his Rhinemaidens should be swimming and singing. *The Ring* in the round would be perfectly feasible with this equipment.' What is more, they had their band suspended on a platform in mid air. Imagine a Wagnerian orchestra playing in the clouds, and being jointly consumed in Valhalla's glorious end. A three-tiered wedding cake – first tier the different sets and preparation, second tier the audience all around the performing arena (with closed-circuit screens for the singers to keep the beat), and the third tier the orchestra and dominating Valhalla set, which should always be present (if screened) to remind us why this dark tale ever unfolded. If ever the Parkinson law that an organization which builds a new headquarters is already dead on its feet has validity, it is in *The Ring*.

October 30

We're doing two performances — tonight it's a diplomatic evening with ministers and bureaucrats. Gill Braithwaite, my hostess, and I spent the day collecting plants for the 'garden'. The Italian Ambassadress has some spectacular rubber plants, so we took a local gang (not unlike Baron Ochs's servants in *Rosenkavalier*) to collect them.

The audience were full of smiles and very receptive. In the pause between Acts 1 and 2, Harry slipped into a chair beside me, his eyes shining. 'Dad, there are masses of tanks drawn up outside!' A real *coup*? A chance to replay my favourite scene in *Carry on up the Khyber*? It was terribly disappointing to find that they were rehearsing for some parade.

November 1

This time it's an artists' audience, chosen by the Ambassador. Not quite so enthusiastic at the beginning, though more so at the end.

'Freddie, I want you to meet . . .'

I was taken across and shook hands with a celebrated Russian director. 'Not much political message in your version,' he said in clipped tones.

'No,' I agreed. 'Except that what I was trying to get across was the futility of Revolution. How all classes could come to terms with each other without slaughter. That's my message.'

He grunted and moved on. The next woman I met still had tears in her eyes. 'I want to thank you all so very much,' she said slowly.

'No, no,' I said. 'It's a great honour to be here.' Indeed, it is.

'But you see,' she said, 'I was the last soprano to sing Susanna in Italian in Moscow. Tonight has brought back so many memories, so much happiness.'

November 5

Back in London and the last night of *Figaro*: cue to keep a beady eye on everyone. There have been some near disasters in the past from practical jokes. At Sledmere, when Norina in *Don Pasquale* is brought a letter to read, she opened the envelope to find nothing but a contraceptive inside. Her attempts to deal with this without laughing were heroic. At Thoresby the Alfredo of the day opened his poetry book to find a simple message 'You're fired' forged with my signature. Walking sticks have been sawn through, stage drinks turned curiously bitter – or worse, a peculiar colour, so that the singer who has to knock one back is convulsed by the fear of what may be in it. The one I liked most was at Barmouth, which has its own joke shop. Bryan and I knew that something was up when we saw two of the cast giggling helplessly in a corner. All through the performance we watched and waited. As the final chorus ended, I turned the last page, and a squidgy red octopus catapulted out and landed on Bryan's lap. He never faltered.

There's a narrow line between permissible last-night fun and something that might actually affect the performance and thus the enjoyment of the audience. No one is amused by a cast who are amusing themselves.

At the end of Act 3, the Count proclaims a party to be held that night. The others are supposed to react with muted enthusiasm.

The singers adore practical jokes.

Tonight they shrieked out their enthusiasm. It was totally plausible to the audience. It nearly threw the Count, but not quite. Everyone brought beer and wine to the party afterwards. Lots of happy reminiscing, and a few tears. We hold the first set of auditions tomorrow.

'See you at nine,' said Bryan, putting on his overcoat. Enid is going back to New Zealand to visit her family, Alice is spending Christmas in Texas, and Helen has a couple of contracts with English National Opera. I shall miss them terribly. But most of the others have signed on. Tomorrow we start looking for a Constanze. And people to employ us.

November 6

The annual End-of-Season Stage Management party. I missed last year's so I postponed a trip to Brittany to come tonight.

Not all the company are here — perhaps twenty singers out of this year's thirty-five; but all the stage management and wardrobe, plus Phyllida and me. I sat between Matt and Amy. Peter held her hand throughout. Bruce Carter, as Stage Manager, gave a masterly speech, recalling the year's best moments and giving out prizes. I was presented with a bottle of vanishing ink 'for the contracts which contribute so much to our overdrafts'. Jubilant applause! Other presentations included a slice of bacon for the hammiest performance and a glued wallet for the meanest spender. The long-service award for Enid, who is leaving, was named after and consisted of a photograph of a girl who was dismissed after a few days for unparalleled idleness. Phyllida got the award for the scantiest underclothes (how did he know?) – a close-run thing, I imagine, in this company. But above all, it was an evening of laughter and relaxation.

Looking round the table at the flushed, happy faces, listening to the uproarious laughter, I couldn't help comparing this with my past life of wet potato fields and stuffy committee rooms. Of course opera is escapism; of course entertainment is a hazardous profession where each of us lives for the day, for the applause, necessarily oblivious of the counter claims of the security of pensionable respectability. But it is also a highly professional and disciplined *métier*, with an end-product for which people will pay. And I wouldn't change it. Our world is no less real than any other. Leoncavallo's *I Pagliacci* ends with the most famous line in all opera:

È finita la commédia.

Ours continues – we hope.